This is a powerful journey that challenges our faith while in the fire and gives us hope knowing that God is moving, even when we don't see it! Prayer works, and G⸱ ⸱ ⸱ ⸱ ⸱⸱

ey
ner

We live in a world that tries to convince us that realness comes only from what we see with our natural eyes. Sadly, many of us have believed it. Shannon's (and Jason's) memoir reminds us that when we seek with our spiritual eyes, God will show Himself to us in ways that we never imagined possible, and in ways we are scarcely capable of understanding. This memoir exudes God's redemptive and healing power that is available to all who believe—and is proof that our worst day can become our greatest testimony.

Katie Moras
Owner, El Bosque Encantado

This is a story of what it looks and feels like to walk the road of faith while believing for the impossible. It is a story of a family whose lives were horribly upended in the blink of an eye and the miracle that so many people got to watch unfold through countless prayers. This book is a beautiful rendering of the faith of a husband, the fight of an incredible woman who refused to give up, and the faithfulness of our mighty God.

As someone who walked this road alongside this family and sat at the hospital during some difficult hours, days, and weeks, my life was impacted by the tenacity of the Kerr family, the beauty of a community of friends, and the power of prayer through every aspect of life. I pray that those who pick up this book are forever impacted as they read about the lifesaving love, grace, and power of Jesus Christ!

Justin Mack
Global Project Pastor, River Valley Church,
Minneapolis, MN

This life, both qualitative and quantitative, can be altered in an instant. The Kerr family tragedy reignites the desire to claim healing and to cling to the expectation that God will show up in spite of what reality appears to be. This book is a true story about faith refined, challenged, and strengthened—like glass being formed in the intense heat of fire. Hope and restoration are themes that God Himself weaves into this journey, using the known and unknown, to fulfill this modern-day miracle.

Kirsten (Kiki) Stapp
Friend and BSN, MS, APRN, CRNA

The Kerrs' story is profoundly moving. As I read this book, I could feel my faith in who God is growing within. Once you start reading this, you won't want to stop. There are moments where things go from bad to worse, but each time God's faithful hand shows up in a dream, a rainbow, a song, a friend, or a stranger in the elevator. It is undeniably a God story. The Kerrs are an incredible picture of God's ability to give us courage and strength under pressure. You'll see that in their weakness God's strength was made perfect.

Ben Markham
Teaching Pastor, Discovery Church, Orlando, FL

Truly a story of heartbreak and triumph. On that fateful day in September, heaven would not get another angel as Shannon has much to accomplish on earth. "I will praise you in this storm." How many tears did God hold in His hand? His cup must have been overflowing. An incredible unwavering faith walk with no doubt left to the reader that the healing hands of God touch the Kerrs. The lives that this story has touched across the world is a true testament of faith.

Janis Barden
Science Teacher and Shannon's Aunt

Everyone, young and old, should read and share with others this incredible true story; it is one of the most heart-wrenching yet miracle-filled journeys that I never expected to witness and experience. It has forever changed my life and has transformed my thoughts and beliefs about God's miraculous healing power, His constant provision, and the true provider of unexplainable peace during times of desperation and despair. This is a powerful testimony of how a family's love and support, as well as unabandoned commitment to pray and hold steadfast to God's promises, can bring about unexplainable miracles. Lastly, this story is a showcase of God's glory, love, and purpose as He shined light through the darkness, answered the prayers of the faithful, and gave hope to the hundreds of thousands that followed along the #TeamKerr journey.

Stephanie Balvin
Thirty-Year Lifelong Friend

A faith inspiring journey about God's grace and mercy when a family is struck by tragedy that could strike any of us. It's encouraging to see how family and friends pull together to intercede and watch God's hand move.

Mark Perryman
Lead Pastor, Northridge Church,
Owatonna, MN

The reality of seeing one of your closest friends on the brink of leaving this world makes you question many things. However, the many miracles that I witnessed during this journey made God and all of His promises come to life. Being a witness to the doctor's prognosis and the reality of what actually happened in this family's journey has been a tangible example of what God can and is doing in this world. His promises are true.

Sara Ryal
Accounting Associate at Lewis & Knopf, CPAs, PC

The story of the Kerr family is sure to stir your faith and capture your heart. Their courage in the face of adversity is played out page by page in this thrilling account of God's grace and miraculous healing power. The intensity of this family's journey can be felt and the clarity of God's hand can be seen in each chapter. Anyone reading this book will leave it with a better understanding of faith and a better idea of how to practically walk that faith out. God truly took ashes and turned them into beauty in this true-life account of what can only be classified as a miracle.

David Hasz
Friend of Jason and Shannon

Shannon's story belongs to all of us. After all, who hasn't been profoundly touched by tragedy at some point in our journeys? What makes Shannon's story unique is the relentless hope that she and her family demonstrated, and their courageous trust that inspired a network of thousands! Read this book prepared to be astounded by God's faithfulness and inimitable ability to bring truth and light to even the darkest circumstances.

Kristi Hedstrom
Family Friend and Author of Shannon's CaringBridge® Page

Against All Odds

An Incredible Journey of Hope and Healing

for Patricia—
May the extraordinary
experience of Shannon
Kerr prompt you to
ponder life from a
fresh perspective. ♡

Lisa Lynn Ericson

Shannon Kerr

with *Lisa Ericson*

bookVillages

ISBN: 978-1-94429-836-4

Cover and interior design by Niddy Griddy Design, Inc.
Ocean photo and wings image © iStock
Interior photos by Kerr Family

Scripture quotations are taken from THE HOLY BIBLE, NEW INTERNATIONAL VERSION®, NIV® Copyright © 1973, 1978, 1984, 2011 by Biblica, Inc.® Used by permission. All rights reserved worldwide.

Holy Bible, New Living Translation, copyright © 1996, 2004, 2015 by Tyndale House Foundation. Used by permission of Tyndale House Publishers, Inc., Carol Stream, Illinois 60188. All rights reserved.

Song Permissions
Oceans (Where Feet May Fail) by Joel Houston, Matt Crocker, Salomon Ligthelm
Copyright © 2013 Hillsong Music Publishing (APRA) (adm. In the US and Canada at CapitolCMGPublishing.com). All rights reserved. Used by Permission.

Anchor by Ben Fielding, Dean Ussher
Copyright © 2013 Hillsong Music Publishing (APRA) (adm. In the US and Canada at CapitolCMGPublishing.com). All rights reserved. Used by Permission.

It Is Well with My Soul by Philip P. Bliss. Public Domain

Whose Report Shall You Believe? By Ron Kenoly, Intregrity Music. Permission requested.

I am Healed by Ryan Williams, KK Brink
Copyright © 2015 Ryan Williams, KK Brink. All rights reserved. Used by Permission.

Look What the Lord Has Done by Mark David Hanby
Copyright © 1974 Capitol CMG Publishing. All rights reserved. Used by Permission.

LCCN: 2018936889
Printed in the United States of America
1 2 3 4 5 6 7 8 9 10 Printing/Year 22 21 20 19 18

I am STILL ALIVE and writing this book ONLY because of Jesus Christ, my Savior. Thank You, Lord.

I dedicate this book to my best friend, dear to my heart, my husband, Jason Michael Kerr. Jason prayed and prayed and prayed and trusted in Jesus. Jason had only faith as he walked this path. Both of our parents whom we call Mom and Dad—my parents, Pat and Shelly McCauley, and Jason's parents, Terry and Kristine Kerr—dropped everything they had going and just came. I love them so much!

Jason spent morning to afternoon with me at the hospital. My dad spent the afternoon and evening with me at the hospital. This was every day. My eyes fill with tears as I type this. I love them!

There is so much to be thankful for. Why focus on the negative? We all can find negatives, but why, when we can choose to focus on the positive that is there. You just have to choose to see it!

Shannon Kerr

Table of Contents

Foreword   11

Acknowledgments   13

The Collision: 15
    September 14, 2015

The Coma: 35
    September 15-November 7, 2015

The Comprehension: 181
    November 8-December 9, 2015

The Clarity: 229
    Epilogue

Foreword

When I heard about the accident, my stomach sank.

"Wait . . . she was with her girls? How bad is it? No, not the Kerrs."

I could picture the intersection of the accident vividly: Castle Rock Intersection—Lakeville, Minnesota. I had driven down those roads many times. Matter of fact, I remember helping out an accident at that exact place on a slippery winter's day a few years ago.

My mind began racing. Maybe it is not as bad as I am hearing. Maybe she just has to go to the hospital as a precaution, but why then would they have to airlift the children, too? As I caught myself in that moment, I was reminded of this: God is in control.

Shannon and her family have been part of our church for years. They have a passion for missions; they love to serve; they give of themselves every day to bring the light of Jesus to those in need. Now they needed us to lift up their hope and faith, and pray for their very lives.

As a pastor, I am no stranger to hospital visits, and this goes down as one of the toughest because not only was Shannon staring down death, but her young girls were also impacted. I remember telling myself, *Don't enter that hospital room without faith. Faith needs to rise up. God is in control.*

I know firsthand God can do the miraculous. My own brother had his own near-death experience and was a survivor—the only logical reason being God intervened.

But when I finally saw her lying in that hospital bed, my faith was on life support just like Shannon was. It was bad—really bad—and I was crushed.

So, I went into chaplain mode. I thought, *I will just focus on caring for her husband, Jason, and the kids. I just need to prepare everyone for her inevitable passing.* In fact, if I could assess my role as pastor in that moment, I was operating with about 10 percent faith and 90 percent family chaplain mode.

But when I talked with Jason, all I heard, all I felt, all I saw was faith, faith, faith. His faith lifted me to hope. He was not showcasing some flashes of wishful thinking. He embodied faith and faith to the fullest. So I did what any good pastor would do—I got behind his faith and pushed with my 10 percent!

The updates started rolling in from the medical staff, and it didn't look good—until the night of our church's live album recording, *Edge of Heaven.*

While we were worshipping that night, I was told Jason was worshipping with us. From the moment Shannon was hospitalized, he had been faithfully juggling husband, dad, business owner, and follower of Jesus. Yet in the midst of all that, he felt a desire to be there because he just needed a night to worship Jesus.

When I went over to him, he was at another faith level, proclaiming Shannon's healing and believing the song we had just sung, "I Am Healed."

I was no longer pushing his faith with the little I had. I was trying to keep up with his faith. He was running with a healing in his spirit and proclaiming it for all to hear!

As you are about to read in this book, something miraculous took place—heaven and earth collided. I pray that if you're at a low percentage spot in your faith, Shannon's story will fire you up and help you believe for more!

Rob Ketterling
Lead Pastor, River Valley Church
Minneapolis, MN

Acknowledgments

First of all, I want to thank our family—the Kerr side, and the McCauley side—for coming from all over the United States to support us. Then I want to thank all our friends. Thank you to River Valley, our church, and all the churches that prayed for me.

People's lives are busy, but our family and good friends dropped everything on that day and came to the hospital! Not only did they come, but they PRAYED! That is real love. I couldn't even ask for help or prayer, but people just came! It means A LOT to me—more than I can even explain.

We also want to thank our publishing team: Susan Blount, Quadrivium Group, for her help and guidance with this book, Karen Pickering, Book Villages, for managing all the details so we have a completed book, and Lisa Ericson for her wonderful writing skills. We have been a

Kerr family picture from before accident

team and couldn't have done this without each one.

We can't even begin to list all the people we would like to thank—the list is enormous. But to each of you, thank you for all your help and making such a difference in our lives
Shannon Kerr

We have so many people to thank for all your prayers and taking the time to come up and sit with us in our journey to our miracle with Shannon. Our family members and extended family that came from Minneapolis, from Michigan, from Arizona, to all our wonderful friends, to our close church families—River Valley and Northridge in Owatonna—your support and prayers meant the world to us!
Shelly McCauley

THE COLLISION
September 14, 2015

The morning was off to a cheerful start, and all three of us were eager to see the Yorkshire terrier puppy that was for sale. Then I looked, turning left at the stop sign, and the carefree, bright sunrise was now shining in my face as I drove east toward Rochester.

It was just my two young daughters, Kyra and Jaydalin, with me, though my oldest son, Trenton, had begged to come along. Yet at age thirteen, Trenton and his nine-year-old brother, Braylon, needed to be in school. Four-year-old Jaydalin would be starting preschool in a few weeks, so she was as free as I was to take this little trip to scout out a puppy on that cloudless morning, Monday, September 14, 2015.

Shannon and girls in van

Kyra was seven and would have been in school that day, like her brothers, except she had injured her hand the night before. We had been to the hospital on Sunday night, a quick dash to the ER at Fairview Ridges Hospital in Burnsville to get some stitches after a freak accident in the kitchen. I had tried to stop it, but it happened too quickly.

That Sunday night, Kyra and I were making chocolate chip cookies for a small crowd of people who were coming to our house for a couples meeting that we call life group. I looked over and saw her sitting on the island countertop where she didn't belong. "Honey, what are you doing?" I said. "Get down."

I had almost finished dropping spoonfuls of cookie dough onto the baking sheet, so Kyra stayed a bit longer on the island to watch. As I put the tray into the oven, she turned obediently to jump down to the floor, holding a glass bowl in her hands. In that instant, our soft-haired English bulldog, Moe, ambled slowly through the kitchen, passing right under Kyra as she was jumping down. She collided with the dog, and the bowl shattered, breaking in her hand. There she was, bleeding, and in just a few minutes our house would be full of guests for our meeting.

After carefully looking at my daughter's injury, I texted a medical professional, asking, "What do I do?" She told me that teary-eyed Kyra would need stitches, so I drove her to the hospital and didn't get back home to Lakeville until 9:30 that night. Meanwhile, my ever-supportive husband, Jason, hosted the crowd who had come to our house as scheduled.

I had planned to meet my mother in Rochester on Monday morning, and from there we would drive more than three hours to a breeder in Wisconsin to look at the sixteen-week-old puppy that I hoped would soon be ours. It was a female dog, and I wanted to train it, like I had been doing with Moe. A Yorkie puppy could be a great addition to our family, something a little cuddlier than our loyal, sturdy bulldog.

It would be worth getting up early for this exciting new venture! That morning as I asked Jason which direction to drive to meet my mother, I wasn't sure what to do about Kyra. Would she be all right in school with fresh stitches in her hand? Jason and I decided that I would take Kyra along with me so that her hand wouldn't be hurting her during all of the activity in school that day. She could rest and be comforted in the van, with her mommy. "Just head down Route 52," Jason told me. "That's the quickest route from here to meet your mom."

I got the boys' lunches ready, made snacks for the girls to take along for the ride, and then went upstairs to wake up the girls. Kyra and Jaydalin came downstairs dressed alike, excited and ready for our ride to see the puppy. They hugged their dad goodbye. Since it was so early, I'd even packed breakfast for them to eat in the van, plus a travel mug of fresh black coffee that I could sip along the way.

I went back upstairs to wake up Braylon. "I will see you after school," I told him. "I'm going to go look at the dog, and I'll pick you up this afternoon." I trotted downstairs to get my shoes and head out the door. Trenton came downstairs too, ready for school. "Son, I love ya!"

Then I left, making sure that the girls were buckled in the back seat of the van, like usual. "Mom, I'm leaving the house," I texted her, and pulled out of the long, curved driveway. It was 7:00 a.m.

I remember going to the first stop sign and turning right, then going straight at the next stop sign. At the last stop sign, I turned left onto 280th Street East, toward Castle Rock. The road was wide open, and we were on our way!

In that instant, the sun in my eyes, I looked and saw nothing, and saw everything. I can't describe it, because I don't really remember it at all.

At the intersection of Highway 3 in Castle Rock, I drove through a stop sign at about 40 mph. I didn't see the sign, nor did I see the semitrailer truck that was fast approaching from the right.

The truck broadsided our van. Jaydalin was sitting behind me, and Kyra was next to her, looking out the window and catching a quick glimpse of the front grille of the truck as it slammed into us at about 60 mph. An ordinary drive, for an ordinary purpose, suddenly became a horribly extraordinary and life-changing event.

Mom's Journal
Today was a horrible day.

Those were the first words that my mother later wrote in her journal, on page 1. Those pages would become a sort of manuscript, telling my story in small glimpses, one day at a time. With the help of other people who saw what happened and experienced it with me, I have been able to piece together a testimony that goes far beyond that horrifying event.

My cell phone automatically called Jason when the weight of my coffee mug pressed the dial button upon impact. All that Jason heard were muffled sounds and a female voice, so he assumed that I had pocket-dialed him. But then he started getting calls from my parents, Pat and Shelly McCauley, wondering where I was. They knew that I'm never late, that I'm always on time for everything. "She should have already been there," he told them. "Something's not right."

Jason had already been to school to drop off Trenton and Braylon. Back at the house, talking with my parents, Jason paused to pray. He remembers, "Here I am, my cell phone on speaker with Shelly and my home phone on speaker with Pat, trying to figure out what we know, which isn't anything." He knew to pray, still not knowing what had happened to me and our girls.

Walking upstairs after a brief workout in the basement, Jason looked at a map. Preoccupied, he decided to leave the house and start driving in the direction where I'd gone. While he was still looking at the map, he got another phone call.

It was a police officer, describing a situation that was not good and asking, "Are these your daughters?" The officer had no identification for the girls in the car.

"Yes, they are," Jason answered, uncertain yet convinced.

"One of them, the older one, and the mom are critical, and it's not good," the officer told Jason. "The other one is coherent. You need to go to the hospital."

Is this real? Jason thought. *The sun is shining, and it's a beautiful Monday morning. They were just here. Are you kidding?*

Jason didn't know what to do. Sweaty and in a rush, he didn't even take a shower—he just left. But then again, he had already done what mattered most. He had prayed. And he sent a group text to friends to say, "Pray. This is what I know. Pray." Then he just started driving to the hospital in downtown Minneapolis.

In his haste, he called my brother Tim, who worked as area manager at Jimmy John's, our franchised sandwich restaurant chain. Normally, Jason would be getting calls from the Jimmy

John's locations that he co-owns with my father. His day was filling up with requests from the managers for him to troubleshoot situations on-site at the various restaurants. But all of that came to a stop with this other phone call, so Tim would have to pass along the message that Jason's day had taken a turn.

While Jason was driving, his mind swirling with human fears yet confident in the sovereign control of his Creator, the same police officer called back. Jason was traveling about 80 mph in the carpool lane, concerned that he might get pulled over for speeding on his fast track to the ER. The officer told him to keep hurrying and to just give the officer's name if anyone pulled him over and questioned him.

As all of this heartrending experience developed, my mother wrote down more of the thoughts she had that day, which became day one of a story that I can't tell by myself. Her own words depicted the desperate cry of a suffering mother.

Mom's Journal

I was supposed to meet Shannon and the girls in Rochester at 8:00 a.m. to go look at a puppy east of La Crosse. They never showed up. At 8:23 a.m., I called Pat and said, "Something is wrong." He called Jason, and we were brainstorming. At 8:45 a.m., I started driving north on 52 to try to see if she broke down and her phone battery was dead. Fifteen minutes later we were talking to Jason, and he said he was getting a call. It ended up being Hennepin County Medical Center telling Jason that they had been in a horrible accident and he needed to get to the hospital ASAP.

I don't remember the stop sign or the truck, nor do I remember much else from that day. The powerful impact of the collision caused severe brain trauma, threatening to suck my very life away, and I was comatose.

As the song "Oceans" by Hillsong United says, *You call me out upon the waters, the great unknown where feet may fail.* I couldn't cry out to God with the words of my favorite song, nor could I even verbalize a prayer. But *in oceans deep my faith will stand,* and countless people upheld me, praying relentlessly. And they recorded what happened as God responded in my unresponsive state. There, true to the lyrics of that song, I found God in the unknowns of a horrifying event that felt like oceans deep. Yet my faith still stands.

Right from the start, on day one, an ordinary day with an ordinary purpose, there are amazing eyewitness accounts that made that day an extraordinary day of miracles—like the man who saw a fourth person at the scene of the accident. Running up to the scene to help, he looked and saw something that none of us can really explain. He saw someone we can only identify as an angel, and he told us about it a few days later. In the unknown, God knows all of it, *and there I find You in the mystery.* It is, in a way, God's triumphant story.

On that fateful day, the collision happened at about 7:15 a.m., and the first responders were at the right place at the right time when they were alerted, allowing them to act quickly.

One of the emergency responders later told us that he was at work one and a half miles away from the intersection in Castle Rock when he received the call. "A few minutes after the page went out, I arrived," he said. The ambulance, with flashing red and blue lights and blaring siren, pulled onto the scene only about ten minutes later, and the same responder asked the attending deputy officer to call a medical helicopter.

By the time the first emergency responder arrived, some passersby had already started helping, taking Jaydalin safely out of the vehicle. She was dazed but coherent, and bystanders had taken her to a grassy plot near the intersection. Only several days later would we hear more about what those emergency responders and bystanders saw inside the van.

In the moment of the collision, my body had shifted violently to the passenger side of the van, and both Kyra and I were trapped inside the vehicle. The passenger door was crushed up against the right side of my head, and I was barely breathing. The emergency responders held my head up so that I could gasp for air, while Kyra cried faintly in the seat behind me. Blood mingled and fused with the fibers of my red shirt, and even little Jaydalin was completely covered in my blood and Kyra's.

The truck driver, who was hauling a full load of beverages, said that he saw the whites in Kyra's eyes a few seconds before impacting my vehicle. He came away from the collision with a broken rib, cuts, bruises, and some stitches, and was soon released from the hospital. The man in the passenger seat of the truck had no injuries at all, and he valiantly acted by spraying the smoking van with the fire extinguisher that they had in the truck. Based on what we heard, the memory of Kyra's face haunted the truck driver and gave him some sleepless nights, but I hope and pray that he has recovered well from the entire incident.

The emergency responders feared the worst for Kyra and me. There was blood-spattered trauma everywhere, and yet they sensed that there was an angelic presence in the atmosphere. They told us that a person was walking around behind them, and no one knew who it was. But whatever they perceived, it was as if peace was hovering over the entire twisted-metal wreckage.

The medical helicopter, with its rotating blades and choppy sound, landed on the road, blocking traffic around the area. Using extraction tools, the emergency crews quickly freed us from the van and transported us by helicopter to Hennepin County Medical Center. According to eyewitness accounts, the entire emergency response and rescue went as smoothly as it could, even faster than expected.

While this was happening, my mother was still trying to find the van and me, somewhere on the roads beyond Rochester. Once the call came from the police officer, my father left my hometown of Owatonna to catch up with my mother in Faribault so that they could go to the hospital together.

The authorities made many unsuccessful attempts to contact my parents and eventually reached them through Facebook. By the time my mother heard the news from Jason, the girls and I had already been admitted to the hospital. My mother penned her thoughts and more details of this distressing ordeal, along with her prayerful outlook.

Mom's Journal

After I got the news, I could hardly breathe! Pat kept telling me to calm down so I didn't have an accident. I then contacted everyone for prayer. I was coming across on 60 heading to Faribault, and there was a detour. I had to go north to Northfield. There was a detour. I had to call Pat to meet me in Elko, and then there was a police officer blocking the road. It ended up being Shannon's accident, so I had to go north. I called Pat again, and he met me at Lakeville Jimmy John's. I drove past the kids' school and prayed for them, knowing that they were going to have to deal with the news.

That day, Jason arrived at the ER at about 10:00 a.m. At first, due to the severity of the injuries and the active medical treatment, he wasn't even allowed to see Kyra or me, only Jaydalin.

Within just twenty minutes, Justin Mack and Greg Youmans, two friends from church, joined Jason at the hospital after receiving his text message. The hospital scene was somewhat chaotic, Justin recalls. Finally they found Jason, just standing there with a confused look, his head between his hands.

"Buddy, it's gonna be OK," Justin said, putting his hand on Jason's shoulder. Jason was tightly holding Shannon's purse, which the medics had handed to him when he walked into the ER.

"Why did they give me her purse?" Jason asked, numbed by the whole scenario.

"I don't know," Justin responded. "Let's pray." Justin sensed that God was strengthening Jason even in that moment, and Greg watched as Jason stepped away from Jaydalin's bed to the window. Spontaneously, Jason kneeled and began to worship and praise

God for who He is—even before knowing the details of what appeared to be an unbearable and inexplicable nightmare.

Justin didn't have a word from God in that instant—no concrete promise that I would be healed. But he felt in his heart that I would be all right. He told Jason that there's not an ounce of give-up in me, saying, "You married a fighter."

It's true that I have always been one to face any competition with pluck. I play to win! I had been a careful driver ever since I got my license and had never been in an accident, even during the sixteen years when I drove for a living as a salesperson for an eye doctor's business. So I was safe behind the wheel but had always been fast on my feet, racing eagerly toward the finish line.

Underneath my competitive spirit is a deep love for people —and for God, who is my only strength. He is the one who made me a fighter, and also a person who loves people. For me, any opponent or any person is first a potential friend, and my conviction is that to live is to love everyone who crosses my path. Little did I know that God would send me the challenge of a lifetime, stopping me dead in my tracks.

Would I live to see another day, to share the prize of God's love? The lyrics of my favorite song were even more poignant now.

Let me walk upon the waters
Wherever You would call me.
Take me deeper than my feet
*   could ever wander*
And my faith will be made stronger
In the presence of my Savior.

As the early, morning cloudless sunrise morphed into the blurry gray of the hospital walls that day, our friends and family began to populate the hallways. These were people whom we loved, who loved us, who came not only out of curiosity but also out of a desire to share a ray of hope. On Sunday, Jason and I had been on the prayer team of our church, praying for people who approached us after the church service. Now, just one day later, people were pouring into this sterile, white space to pray for us, to offer the warmth of their loving care.

My friend Kiki Stapp was one of many who arrived at the hospital, asking about me. "I need that woman," Jason told Kiki. "Just pray."

Another friend, Mandy Spinler, called my mother while my parents were driving to the hospital. "It's bad," my mother told her. Mandy stopped what she was doing at home and prayed with her husband, then kept pacing and praying as the minutes and hours continued.

While she was praying, Mandy had a vision of me speaking to a group of ladies. It was a very brief vision, but she saw that my hair was long and blonde, and I was walking on a stage as I spoke. "Thank You, Jesus," Mandy uttered. At the time, amid that ethereal vision, all she knew was that it had been a bad accident and that the girls and I had been urgently airlifted by helicopter.

Mandy shared what she believed to have been a divine vision with my mother right away. "It was so special that God gave us that hope," Mandy said. "Because medically there was no hope."

And all of this was unfolding before we had even heard about the extra person, yes, that fourth person in the van—the angel—who had been on the scene during the crash. It would be a few days before that news would reach my family.

As my mother saw it, there were miracles from the start.

Mom's Journal

We finally got to the hospital, and our first miracle was that they were all alive! Jaydalin was good, just glass cuts and a small concussion. Kyra was critical and so was Shannon. But they're alive—and critical but stable. They both had ventilators to help them breathe. Shannon ended up having surgery to remove a portion of her skull so her brain could expand.

My head was severely smashed, and the medical staff had to insert a probe in my head to test the brain pressure. Jason had to sign off on the procedure. However, medical personnel came back quickly, saying that they had to relieve the pressure as soon as possible. That meant taking off part of my skull.

Best case is that she will be a vegetable, Jason thought fearfully. *They are removing part of her skull, and she's barely breathing. This is not good.*

Doctor talking to Jason, Dad, Mom and two brothers

Jason couldn't mentally process what the doctors were telling him, nor could he comprehend what medical releases he was signing. As he chose to trust that they knew what they were doing, Jason turned to my father and said, "I'm signing to create a vegetable right now."

It was all becoming an agonizing, swirling blur, steadied only by the assurance that God was in control. As minutes and hours began to pass in the hospital, my family realized that the news would spread quickly, and they wanted to be sure that the boys didn't hear about it from someone else or from social media. Who would break this devastating news to Trenton and Braylon? My brother Tim took that hard job, going to the boys' school to pick them up and tell them what had happened.

When Tim arrived at the school, the boys were excited, thinking that he was coming because of the puppy. Tim said little. "Your mom had an accident, and she is hurt, and you need to go with me to the hospital." The boys were stunned, grappling with this twist of events.

Jason would have to fill them in on the details. Trenton and Braylon walked into the hospital at about 1:00 p.m., approaching their father and saying, "Dad, what happened to Mom?"

I was in surgery when they arrived, so the boys didn't see me at first. They started with visiting Jaydalin because their little sister was conscious, watching a movie in her hospital bed. The

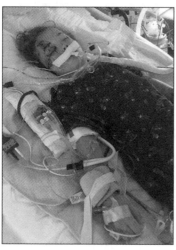

boys' unbreakable sibling bond with their little sister was a gift to their hearts as they lived the incomprehensible situation of their visit to the hospital.

Jaydalin had suffered a mild concussion and was talking, saying, "Daddy, I've got to go with Mommy to see the puppy." Jaydalin's confusion didn't diminish her spunky spirit too much, and by the end of the day she was quietly playing with Play-Doh in her hospital bed.

Kyra in coma

Kyra was next door to Jaydalin in the pediatric ICU, with injuries to her lungs, liver, pelvis, and head, but she was stable. The medical personnel skillfully sedated Kyra in an induced coma and ventilated her, allowing her body to recover under close watch. They performed brain scans and found nothing alarming.

While the boys were still at the hospital, I came out of surgery, and they got to see me. Fragile and yet fighting for my life, I was surrounded by a maze of tubes and cords, my head covered with protective bandages. My eyes were closed, and the only thing blinking in the room were the screens monitoring my vital signs. Comatose, I was in no condition to recognize my sons, and no one can imagine how difficult that

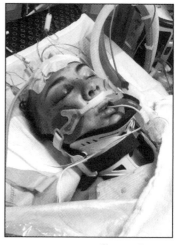

Shannon in coma

visit was for them. Trenton later said to us, "You took me out of the worst class that I had that day to give me the worst news."

Jason encouraged the boys to hold my hand, limp as it was, the same hand that just hours before had packed their lunches. In that moment of stunned silence, as Trenton and Braylon stared at their mom, Jason said, "Listen, whether we are at the water park today or at the hospital, we stop to pray." The boys knew that, and they prayed, verbalizing with the simple words yet strong faith of a child, trusting that God could make things better. The boys' prayers in the very critical circumstance grew their faith and strengthened the bonds of our family.

That appeal for prayer resounded not just in the privacy of our family's struggle, but also in every message that Jason issued. Soft-spoken on the surface, my husband was not at all timid about asking people to pray.

Our friend Kristi Hedstrom became a messenger, too, pleading with others to join my family in praying for healing. She was only two blocks away from the hospital when she received a text message from her mother, Karen, telling her that my daughters and I had been in a really serious accident. Kristi is like family to us, and the news gripped her heart. Within minutes, Kristi walked to the hospital, where many of my family members were already gathered. "It was just surreal," Kristi told me afterward.

A doctor came to the pediatric ICU to give a report to Jason, and Kristi stood nearby. Wanting to be helpful, she whipped a little notepad out of her purse and began to jot down what the doctor was saying so that Jason wouldn't have to try to remember everything in the state of shock that hung over the bleak scene. As other friends started arriving, Kristi read her notes to people, wanting to keep the medical facts straight. My father even asked her for a copy of those pages in her notepad so that he could accurately repeat what the doctor had said.

As Kristi observed that more and more friends were calling and sending text messages to my family, she spoke with my mother, offering to create a CaringBridge® site so that everyone could know what was happening. My mother liked the idea, but told Kristi to check with Jason.

Purposeful though not wanting to interrupt Jason as he focused on my condition, Kristi asked my husband. Jason said, "Is it going to make people pray, Kristi?" She nodded. "Then, yeah, that's fine." Kristi then asked him if he wanted her to set the website for public or private use. "To this," Jason replied, "I want as many people praying as possible."

Kristi stayed throughout the day at the hospital, watching as Jason prayed for a doctor before signing a consent form, and taking more notes after talking with a nurse. Then, midafternoon, she asked the hospital staff if there was a computer she could use, and they directed her to the library downstairs. Kristi had read CaringBridge® posts before but had never set up an account. She figured out how to navigate the site, and within forty-five minutes, the first post was established, with a boldly appropriate heading: *Pray for the Kerr Family!* In just a few lines, Kristi summarized the collision and our medical status, then when on to say:

CaringBridge® Blog
Jason is asking for prayer, prayer, and more prayer for his family. We are trusting God to heal and sustain life in this situation. Please join the Kerr and McCauley families in praying for a complete recovery for all three Kerrs! Please also pray for healing for the driver of the semitruck, who sustained non-life-threatening injuries. We will update this site as more news emerges. Thank you for your prayers, love, and support!

A couple of hours later, Kristi checked the CaringBridge® site, and already there were about 5,000 hits. She thought that statistic must be for the entire website, but then realized that it wasn't. Thousands of people had tuned into that one post.

That post at 3:49 p.m. on Monday was the first of a series that Kristi faithfully managed for us. She approached it like a reporter and tried to reflect our mind-set as well as our faith in everything she wrote. Playing the part of a journalist, she researched the medical terms and checked her facts, wanting to be sure that every detail she shared was accurate. Her role spared Jason of having to keep repeating everything that the doctors were telling him. He would tell Kristi what he knew, confident that she would communicate with the countless readers in a way that upheld his perspective on the whole scenario. Sometimes she was at the hospital once or twice a day to hear the reports directly from the doctors.

To her advantage, Kristi is calm in a crisis, so she was able to handle the intensity of the immediate emergency, and she took the ongoing responsibility seriously. In the beginning, she posted updates at least twice a day, then once a week, then with less frequency—but always faithfully. "I was there, and I was invested," Kristi later told my family. "I wanted to help, and I wanted to represent the family because I love them so much, and I love Shannon."

Understanding that my family was entrusting this crisis to God, Kristi decided to not only emphasize prayer but also add Scripture verses to the posts. The first verses were Psalm 103:1–5:

> Praise the LORD, my soul;
>> all my inmost being, praise his holy name.
> Praise the LORD, my soul,
>> and forget not all his benefits—
> who forgives all your sins
>> and heals all your diseases,
> who redeems your life from the pit
>> and crowns you with love and compassion,
> who satisfies your desires with good things
>> so that your youth is renewed like the eagle's.

I wasn't awake to pick those verses, but Kristi got it right with her choice. Even though I couldn't express any thoughts at all, deep in my soul I knew that only Jesus is able to heal. And He had redeemed my life. Just like the song "Oceans" says, *You've never failed and You won't start now.* Kristi shared that faith with anyone who read the CaringBridge® site, and the prayers of faith began to multiply.

People were posting comments on the site like crazy, and some of the readers were complete strangers. "I was on that road that day, and I saw the ambulances," someone said. "I was praying for Shannon." And others would mention their international location, commenting, "I'm praying from India."

The word also got out quickly to our relatives and friends across the country. My aunt Peggy, my father's oldest sister in North Carolina, started praying as soon as she got a phone call with the devastating news. As she was praying, she had an amazing vision. With eyes of faith, she looked up and saw Jesus on the left, looking down to talk with me. In her vision, I was kneeling, and my hair was long—not like the bristly crew cut after they shaved it in the surgical room. Aunt Peggy watched as I was being told to decide whether or not I wanted to stay alive in my earthly body. Jesus was saying to me, "If you stay, you will have to fight. It won't be instantaneous." My spirit had already gone up, but in the vision I chose to go back and keep living on earth.

In the midst of our desperate crisis, people like Aunt Peggy were bombarding heaven with prayer, and their faith was contending against the medical prognosis. We were all in this battle together. "Shannon needs to keep fighting," Aunt Peggy said. "Shannon's spirit knows to fight even though she is in a coma."

Liz Matson, Peggy's daughter-in-law, was another person who stopped what she was doing as soon as she heard about the accident that day. Before Liz even knew how severely injured I was, she was praying and trusting that I would come out of it. "It looked bad," Liz later said. "But we pled our case before God, and we didn't give up. It was a long fight." Aunt Peggy's vision was right—the results weren't instantaneous.

This was only day one, and I was incoherent for about seventy-two days. But I was alive!

Jason remembers the first night in the hospital, going from room to room to room, his wife and two girls in intensive care. The Kerr family was in catastrophic crisis, and he was husband and father, unable to make the agony go away. He was walking back to the pediatric ICU and pushed the button at the entrance, waiting to be admitted to the restricted area. In that instant, he felt a peace come over him. "It was the peace that surpasses understanding," Jason said. It was a peace that assured him of God's hand over the entire situation.

Jason's thoughts became a prayer. *I am exactly where You want me to be right now, with this turmoil and destruction in my family, and I can rest in that.* The peace Jason experienced didn't make any sense to him at an earthly level—it was a spiritual reality. "The peace of God, which transcends all understanding, will guard your hearts and your minds in Christ Jesus" (Philippians 4:7). God's peace, God's presence, put the distress into perspective. Jason was certain that God was caring for his family, with firm control over the day and all the unexpected trauma that had unfolded. His girls were in intensive care, and Jason was right there, too, walking into the ICU as the doorway opened, confronting the new reality.

The initial procedure to cut away part of my skull was successful in stopping the bleeding. With my head now opened, my brain was acutely swollen and in need of pressure relief.

Everyone else was looking for relief, too. My mother put that yearning into words, alongside a word of faith.

Mom's Journal

The first night was scary! Nobody got much sleep. I was up by 4:00 a.m., walking and praying for you, Baby Girl. I love you so much. I just keep praying for God's restoration for every brain cell in your brain. Rest in Jesus!

THE COMA

September 15, 2015 through November 7, 2015

"Your prayers for Kyra have been answered," the neurosurgeon told my family the next day. The doctors were pleased with the responsiveness of my daughter Kyra's brain and were already talking about the possibility of taking her off the sedation medication within a matter of hours. Later that day they inserted a feeding tube, and she was already beginning to breathe on her own with minimal assistance from the ventilator. She was still in an induced coma, though; her hardy but delicate little seven-year-old body was balancing on a seesaw of life and death.

After being sleepy on Monday, Jaydalin was already bouncing back, with the likelihood that she would be released on Wednesday. She started vomiting at 6:30 a.m. and threw up three times Tuesday morning, which is a typical aftereffect of trauma, but by 9:30 a.m., she was back to her normal self. The only reason that Jaydalin remained in the pediatric ICU that second day was because it kept her close to Kyra, which made it easier for my family to be with both of my children. The doctors continued to monitor Jaydalin, and by the end of the day, the speech and occupational therapists gave her the necessary clearances to go home.

More people were gathering from far away, including Jason's parents, Terry and Kristine Kerr, who had flown in to Minneapolis from Michigan late on Monday night. They arrived at 11:00 p.m. and slept in Kyra's hospital room, while my mother and Karen Hedstrom slept by Jaydalin's side. Throughout the night, Jason and my father had stayed near my bed, taking turns to watch me closely, looking for any sign of responsiveness.

The recovery progress of the girls was sobered by the fact that I was still in a coma. My vital signs were stable, but my motionless body showed no trace of the active athlete that I had been not long ago.

As Tuesday morning dawned, the bright daylight meant little

inside the sterile, white hospital walls, and nothing much had changed. The computer monitors with the little green lights tracking my status continued to rhythmically issue the sad beep, beep, beep, like the steady minutes on a clock, as my family stood by my bedside, waiting for my body to revive. Reality was sinking in—the severity of my injuries was staggering. Yet in that agonizing stillness, encouraging messages rang loudly with hope through the silence.

Terry, my father-in-law, received a text message from a friend, a retired church pastor, assuring him that God would use people of faith to accomplish great things through this crisis. Moments later, Jason asked his father, "Dad, do you think God caused this to happen?"

"I think God allowed it because He's going to use it," Terry said.

My mother, too, had a strong sense that God was in the process of doing great things, right from the start. Her sister Jani had flown in from Phoenix at 12:30 a.m., and the two of them began talking about the small glimmers of God's triumph that were already shining on the scene.

It was Aunt Jani who gave my mother the journal. My mother, who normally only journals when she goes on a trip, had a distinct urge to write down what was happening. In the dim outlook of my condition, which contrasted with the glaring fluorescent lights reflecting from the white hospital walls, my mother looked intently and saw God at work. "I don't want to forget it," she said, "and I want Shannon to know."

My mother's jottings didn't go into much detail—just enough to prompt curiosity and to trigger a memory. As the weeks wore on, she was very busy as a substitute mother to my children, and most of the time she was writing in her journal in the dark, tucked in bed next to Jaydalin. "But it was important to me that I had something written down," my mother later said. She did it for me, and without realizing it, she did it for the many people who would later learn more about what God did, day by day, page by page.

Mom's Journal
The words the Lord gave us today. Karen went in and prayed with Shannon at 4:00 a.m., and He gave her three things:
1. Something about His arm.
2. He was sovereign.
3. He was doing a work that we couldn't see right now.

He also gave her the words to the song "Oceans." We told Jason this, and he said that was Shannon's favorite song. So that song has become our song of encouragement.

It was incredible that on this day when my family was thirsty for good news, God had washed an ocean of comfort over our friend Karen Hedstrom with the words to the very song that had become my favorite. I had first heard "Oceans" in September of 2014, one year before the accident, while in the southern African country of Swaziland with Jason and a team from our church. We would sing it at the hotel during our team meetings, sitting around in a circle. The song had touched my heart on the other side of the ocean, on a ministry trip to Africa, where its compelling lyrics seemed to echo the faith in God that had carried me there. My faith in Jesus is my life, and that song became a voice for my soul. *When oceans rise, my soul will rest in Your embrace, for I am Yours and You are mine.*

Jason already knew that "Oceans" was special to me, and he knew that the song had also touched Kyra that summer. One Saturday evening in July as the sun was setting with dim roseate rays, our family was in the van, looping around Minneapolis on Interstate 494 after going to a birthday party, and the song was playing on the radio. *And my faith will be made stronger in the presence of my Savior.* Hearing it, Kyra was moved deeply by the presence of God, with tears streaming down her cheeks. When the song ended, Kyra said, "The Lord was with me." That realization would become even more meaningful several weeks later, after she survived the accident. God was with her in that same van, both times, in a way that we can hardly explain. Dimmed roseate rays of the sun can be a sunset or a sunrise. God is in both.

So, while Kyra and I were each still in a coma, Jason would kneel next to our hospital beds and play "Oceans" from his cell phone. Once, when Jason was playing the song in Kyra's room, some doctors entered, determined to proceed with their medical duties. The head nurse was standing nearby and stopped them, recognizing that it was a wonderful moment between father and daughter—and God. *So I will call upon Your name and keep my eyes above the waves.* "No, wait," she told them, and they paused their activity until the song had finished. It was amazing what the nurse was sensing. *And my faith will be made stronger in the presence of my Savior.*

My family kept trusting that there was something bigger taking place, beyond what they could see on the surface. It was heartening that others around them were detecting that as well, clues that pointed toward God's good and mysterious ways amid the all-encompassing pain that gnawed at their hearts. As my mother says, "We were walking through everybody's nightmare as a family." My family knew that God was taking them by the hand and walking with them, hour by hour, giving them the strength to put one foot in front of the other.

Maintaining a peaceful perspective was challenging for Jason and my whole family as they were inundated by medical reports. The doctors' assessments were dire, based on the data that they had available, and their communications contrasted with the confidence that God was going to put me back on my feet again.

The doctors were talking about brain damage, while Jason was longing to simply hear more about how God created the human brain, speaking it into existence, healing any damage with His touch. Just several weeks before the accident, a cognitive neuroscientist named Dr. Caroline Leaf had spoken at our church. We had been fascinated by her descriptions of how intricate the human brain is, crafted by God's hands. Jason later realized how timely her presentation had been, preparing him to face the ramifications of my brain injury with greater awareness of how the human mind is wired.

The medical staff at Hennepin County Medical Center is highly skilled, and traumatic brain injury is something that they know how to address, to the best of their ability. The doctors were right in determining that I had suffered a devastating brain injury. There were three neurosurgeons sharing my case, and they tried their hardest to understand the extent of my brain damage and to resuscitate me. As one of them later confided, "There was no giving up." But also, there was no denying the fact that my neurofunction was not good at all.

In the midst of an atmosphere influenced by a grim medical prognosis, Jason chose to cling to the peace that God had conveyed to him, beyond what any mind could invent. And with that, Jason trusted that God is the ultimate healer.

Jason thought, *I've got two family members whose lives are hanging. Only my Savior can change this. There's no physical fix, no doctor, no hospital, not even any hocus-pocus that can help.*

"Being religious increases resilience," one of the doctors said. "It can only help." Noticing that I always had people around me, they also told us that my positive family environment was a boost to my recovery. In addition, I had a throng of prayerful visitors.

At least a hundred people came by the hospital within the first day. It was overwhelming for Jason to have a procession of concerned visitors looking in on a situation where there were so many questions and so few answers. He wished he could say to each of them, "Thanks for coming. I don't really need you to be here—I just need you to pray."

I love people! And I love to pray! I am so glad that the people came, and that they prayed, too. Jason, my family, my friends—everyone did the best thing they could have done by entrusting me to God's care. It was hopeless for them to try anything else because Jesus is our only hope. Jason was hosting a crowd of people at an event that no one would ever really want to attend. He was grateful for their concern, but casual conversation seemed pointless. It was no party. So he said to one person after another, "Use your energy to pray." And that's exactly what they did.

My mother heard again that day from Aunt Peggy in North Carolina.

Mom's Journal

Peggy called and said she had a breakthrough in prayer. She was filled with peace and that we were going to start seeing good things happen. Amen.

The people and the prayers kept coming. Our friends Ben and April Markham flew up from Florida, arriving on Tuesday and staying for six days. We had been newlyweds together when the four of us lived in Michigan and have stayed in close contact ever since. Jason had texted Ben on Monday, saying, "There's been an accident. Please pray." As Ben and April started to grasp the gravity of the situation, they looked at their savings and scraped together enough to book airline flights, bringing their two young boys along. They arrived and announced, "We're here to help with the kids." And they were here to pray alongside us.

A friend of the Markhams had tried to warn them how tough it would be to see me in my condition. But seeing something in person is not the same as hearing about it. Ben later told us, "When I saw Shannon for the first time, it was devastating." Pristine white sheets enveloped my listless body while an inflatable covering regulated my temperature and a protective shell encased my shattered skull. "She didn't look like a human anymore," Ben said. "There was no trace of her, the swelling was so severe."

"When I first walked in to see Shannon," April said, "she was not recognizable, only her nose." And yet, that was not her only first impression.

April looked, and there was something else that caught her eye, somewhere above the pure white sheets and against the orange wall that served as a warm backdrop to my frailty. "When I went to see Shannon, in the empty space at the top of her bed, I saw an angel with huge wings stretched out." April said that every time she walked into my room during those six days, God's presence was so strong. In the midst of her immense grief, bewildered to see me unconscious, April said there was an overall peace that had nothing to do with the silence of my coma. "I knew that God would work it out for good," she said.

God, these kids need their mom, April thought. As she had intended, she helped with the kids, organizing rides and food along with others who were delivering snacks to the hospital. "Jason didn't want to eat," April said. "He was so steadfast, a rock."

Jason was not alone in his rock-solid faith, and friends like Ben and April understood the spiritual dimension of what was happening in our crisis. Ben prayed and read Scripture by my bedside, paging through pretty much any account of healing in the Gospels.

Meanwhile, all the people were wailing and mourning for her. "Stop wailing," Jesus said. "She is not dead but asleep." They laughed at him, knowing that she was dead. But he took her by the hand and said, "My child, get up!" Her spirit returned, and at once she stood up. Then Jesus told them to give her something to eat. (Luke 8:52–55)

I was still unresponsive, and Ben admits that it was so difficult looking for a response that wasn't happening. But as Jason says, "Praise Jesus even when it's hard." And people like Ben and April were there to do that.

"We had some of the most precious times of worship that we had ever experienced," Ben said. April sang "Oceans" to me a cappella, her beautiful voice gently declaring the faith that I couldn't verbalize. Spirit, lead me where my trust is without borders. Let me walk upon the waters wherever You would call me.

I had no idea that my journey with God would take me beyond the borders of the racetrack, beyond the boundary lines of the basketball court, where I had excelled in high school, to a walk of faith like this. Here there was no trophy-winning speed, only stillness. I couldn't even walk at all, and I couldn't sing those lyrics from my hospital bed. But I like to think that my ears heard that music as April sang, and my heart listened in agreement. My trust in Jesus needed to be without borders if my motionless body would ever walk upon the waters.

Wrapped in crisp hospital linens, my vital signs monitored every second, my heart and soul still had faith in Jesus, and my family and friends were surrounding me with unconditional love and care on this journey. Beyond that, as the days went on, we became more and more aware that there were angels with us. I was not alone in my struggle. "Therefore, since we are surrounded by such a great cloud of witnesses, . . . let us run with perseverance the race marked out for us, fixing our eyes on Jesus" (Hebrews 12:1-2). While I lay there, severely injured in my hospital bed, eyes closed, I needed others to keep their eyes on Jesus for me.

For those who had their eyes open, there was a lot to see. April was driving to the hospital within the first three days of the accident and, looking upward, saw a rainbow. It was completely unexpected, an impression of God in that moment, as she approached the intensive care unit to face again the destructive aftermath of the accident. Seeing the rainbow reminded her of the promises of God to Noah after the devastating flood. "Never again will all life be destroyed by the waters of a flood; never again will there be a flood to destroy the earth" (Genesis 9:11). The accident had felt like a flood, but maybe it was an ocean of teeming waters where we would soon be walking high above the waves.

For now, though, it was only day two, and we still had a lot of ground to cover in the hospital. Aside from people like Ben and April who came from out of town, my local friends also immersed themselves in the torrent, showing up and doing anything they could to alleviate the discomfort of keeping vigil in the ICU. The hospital allowed my family access to a private room where they could sit and wait. My parents called it their concrete bunker. The stress level for my family was off the charts because they were the only ones who really knew the severity of my condition. Kristi Hedstrom had been careful not to post anything overly alarming on the CaringBridge® site.

Mandy, who has been my friend since we were in fourth grade together in my hometown of Owatonna, and who was close enough to know what was happening, wheeled a cartload of goodies into the waiting area. She even brought a coffee machine. She and some of my other friends who had known me since childhood would sit with my family during those long hours. A sip of steaming hot coffee, comforting conversations, and hopeful prayers were the order of the day.

My father remembers those visits, as time plodded along while I lay there in a coma. "Shannon has a lot of friends, and they are just wonderful," he said. My childhood friends hadn't seen my parents for many years, so they were not only bringing cookies, they were telling stories from the past. "There were no secrets left," my father later told me with a smile. "All of the sneaking out of the house and everything was all laid out while Shannon slept."

After asking permission from my family, Mandy also took pictures, not to post publicly but to compile a memory book. "One day, you'll want these," she told my parents. Knowing me well, Mandy was sure that I would want to know the nitty-gritty of my condition, not the candy-coated version. She was right—I love chocolate, but when it comes to talking about life, don't sweeten it for me. I like to know what is real. And my comatose reality wasn't pretty as I slept through everything happening around me.

Kiki, a close friend from church who had also been to the hospital on day one, came back right away on Tuesday, this time with a framed photo of Jason and me. It had been taken on Saturday night, only about thirty-six hours before the accident. Kiki, her husband, Ben, Jason, and I had gone to a swing dance at an airport hangar, and someone snapped a photo of all four of us together. She cropped the image so that it was just the two of us—Jason, standing tall in a white shirt, black pants, and suspenders, with a wide-brimmed hat plopped whimsically on his head, his hand casually tucked in his pocket, and me, wearing a simple, short-sleeved, red dress, leaning close to my husband, my hand against his chest, my long blonde hair tumbling well past my shoulders. We were all smiles.

The photo had captured our untarnished bliss, and only the pale green frame was slightly distressed with chipped paint, for artistic effect. But that was Saturday night, and now it was Tuesday. My life now seemed to be the opposite, framed as I was by exquisite medical technology, my body flat on the bed. The injuries had totally changed my appearance, and I was obviously not dancing, nor was my hair bouncing happily with the music.

"I put the photo in Shannon's room at the hospital so that the medical team caring for her could see it," Kiki said. "I wanted to humanize Shannon and show them how vivacious she was." The doctors could only see an injured woman, and my friend wanted them to see who I really am. Kiki wanted to set before them an image of not just who I had been, but who I could be again.

Not only did Kiki know me as a swing-dancing friend who could make a comeback, she also knew that God would be the one to accomplish that. On one of the days after the accident, when she was praying, Kiki had a vision. "Shannon was walking back and forth on a stage, speaking to a large group of people," Kiki said. "She was preaching, very animated with her arms." I had never been a public speaker, so this was definitely a new insight. No one knew at the time how that vision would materialize, but even in those early days of my unconsciousness, God was making it clear that amazing things were on the horizon.

Having a confident hope like this didn't come easily to someone like Kiki. She works in the medical field at Abbott Northwestern Hospital in Minneapolis, so she was well aware that my status was grim. "Knowing what I know," Kiki said, "she shouldn't have made it." But, of course, Kiki also knew God!

Along with the swing-dance photo, Kiki brought a small,

framed chalkboard that was propped up on a little easel, placing it on a shelf near the window in my hospital room, where people could take turns writing verses from the Bible. She took the lead, printing in white, bright green, and cheerful pink, "Be strong and courageous. Do not be afraid; do not be discouraged, for the LORD your God will be with you wherever you go" (Joshua 1:9).

That same day, Anastasia brought a radio so that I could have uplifting music in the background. The photo of the real me, the Bible verse, and the music created a great setting to support my recovery. Right away, and on a regular basis, Kiki played the hymn "It Is Well with My Soul" from her cell phone.

When peace, like a river, attendeth my way,
When sorrows like sea billows roll;
Whatever my lot, Thou hast taught me to say,
It is well, it is well with my soul.

I am sure that those soaring vocals touched my soul. On a lighter note, Kiki also played a video that I had recorded on Saturday night at the swing dance. Jason and Ben were playing instruments at the event, and it had been such a fun moment for me. Afterward, I had sent that video to my friends, saying, "I love that man." When I got out of my coma, I asked to see that video!

With bittersweet memories of a swing dance that had come to a full stop, life had lost its cadence. Little Jaydalin's bright disposition in the hospital made the entire experience just a little bit easier. Her smile was what my family needed to see during those first couple of days.

At one point, Jaydalin said, "I wish I could be there instead of Kyra." My family thought it was so sweet that Jaydalin would trade places with her sister, who had taken a stronger blow from the impact of the collision. But actually, Jaydalin was wishing that she could have all of the attention—and all of the candy that she wanted!

The girls were receiving great care by the hospital staff.

The pediatric ICU nurses were so good with the kids, and they obviously loved their jobs. They were trained in how to handle the uncertainties of medical situations in a way that put the children more at ease. The nurses even helped Trenton and Braylon adjust to seeing their sister Kyra when she was still in an induced coma. Her head was swollen; her hair matted with blood that had dried. It was a scary scene not fit for the eyes of any older brother, making Jaydalin's smile seem that much more important to cheer her brothers.

Jaydalin was thrilled when Kristi's father, Gary Hedstrom, brought her blanket to the hospital. She had been asking to have it with her, the fuzzy fleece and cheery pattern acting as a comforting companion. Gary and his wife, Karen, are not only long-term friends from Owatonna, he is also our insurance agent. Gary went to inspect the van on Tuesday and, peering inside the metal shell that remained, saw a few of our belongings strewn around. It would be a few more days before my family would hear another eyewitness account from someone else who had looked inside a few seconds after the collision. Gary brought back to Kristi's apartment some items that he had salvaged from the wreckage, including both Kyra's and Jaydalin's blankets. He spent a long time kneeled on the kitchen floor, picking shards of glass off the blankets and treating the bloodstains with a chemical cleaner before tossing them in the washing machine.

Seeing her cherished blanket when Gary brought it to her, Jaydalin exclaimed, "This is MY blankie!" Her expression was more than enough reward for the ugly task of cleaning up the blood. Gary's loving gesture had been a grueling job, and it would have been so much harder for Jason to crouch over that sickening mess. Gary is a father, too, and he was willing to get his hands dirty so that somebody's little girl could have her blanket.

So there was the comfort of a soft, familiar blanket, and there was the steady, gentle comfort that God sent to embrace my family as they waited in the hospital, sitting in that concrete bunker.

Mom's Journal

Mike Ramsey had a word.

I am here.
Call My name and I am here.
Call My name and I will walk with you.
Call My name and I will stand with you.
Call My name and if need be I will carry you.
Call My name and I am here.

Mike Ramsey is my brother Mike's father-in-law. The words that he shared with my mother were a huge comfort. His friendship with our family and his understanding of God were a lifeline for us.

Now it was day three. My mother marked off the days in the pages of her journal, not knowing how high she would have to be counting.

Karen Hedstrom and my mother helped to hold down the vigil with Kyra and me. Watching over us was emotionally draining, but they felt God's strong presence and the support of so many people who were praying tirelessly.

Even the state highway patrol officer dropped by the hospital to check on how the girls were doing. Jaydalin was fully alert, dressed in a turquoise T-shirt and sitting in a chair. The two tiny bandages on the inside of her elbows where the nurses had drawn blood for testing were a subtle hint that despite her wide grin, she had been through a lot in the past couple of days.

When the officer arrived, wearing the black pants and beige shirt of his uniform, his hair trimmed short, Jaydalin promptly asked him, "Where's your hat?" She had remembered seeing it on the morning of the accident! The officer raised his hand from his side, gripping the hat and placing it on Jaydalin's head. Her grin was even wider in that moment.

Jaydalin was discharged from the hospital in the afternoon. Before she left, the nurses told my family to keep her calm at home. *Good luck with that one!* my mother thought. Once she was back at our house, Jaydalin began running and playing like usual. After all that she had endured, no one really wanted her to be anything but a lively, joyful four-year-old.

Jeff and Sarah Ryal showed up at our house in Lakeville, pitching in to keep things going for the boys, and now Jaydalin. Jeff and Jason had met when they were nine-year-old boys in Michigan and grew up together. After we were married, Jason and I lived in Michigan, where he and Jeff formed a business partnership, working together as carpenters until the financial crisis of 2008, which meant that people weren't putting a dime into home improvement projects. As that unfolded, Jeff decided to follow God's leading into full-time mission work, and in 2009, our family moved back to Minnesota to pursue another business. By that time, we had three kids. Although Jason and Jeff had cut off their business partnership, their close connection never ended.

The boys' school schedule and sports activities required a constant flow of shuttling back and forth. Jeff sketched out a calendar, coordinating schedules with the school principal and other parents in the community so that there was always a ride. And Jeff didn't forget that growing boys need food, so he came loaded with snacks, prepared to pack lunches.

Many other friends were helping at the same time. The food just kept coming and coming to our house, cooked by people who knew that we're in the habit of eating healthy food. They shopped at our favorite health food store, spending more money to be sure that the ingredients were top quality. At first, the boys felt a little surprised by the constant abundance of food, but then they realized that it was all an attempt to fill the gap in my absence.

Trenton later told me, "Well, the food they brought wasn't as good as your cooking, but some of it was really good. I really liked the pasta." Somehow, thanks to our friends, there was fresh food in the refrigerator, fresh laundry in the mudroom, and fresh water in the dog's bowl. The refreshing presence of friends sustained a house that wasn't the same without Mom. It was exactly what we needed.

Meanwhile, Kyra was slowly improving. The doctor discovered some fluid on her lung, so they drained it and kept her on the ventilator. They also gradually worked toward weaning her off the sedation medication, awaiting an assessment by the neurosurgeon. With the decreased medication, Kyra was even able to respond to some verbal commands. Her brain was still under the effects of the trauma and the induced coma, but any progress was a move in the right direction.

All three of my younger brothers were rallying for me, joining the vigil at the hospital and watching to see the spunk of their older sister return. Though most people call them Dan, Tim, and Mike, they are forever my little brothers—Danny, Timmy, and Mikey John. Dan took a turn at the computer, posting his thoughts on the CaringBridge® site. He wanted to introduce all of the readers to the Shannon McCauley Kerr that he knows.

CaringBridge® Blog
Shannon is the oldest of four kids. She was the only girl. She stood her ground when it came to her younger brothers. Michael, Tim, and I were blessed to have an older sister growing up. Even though she was a girl, not one of us would try to take her on in, well, pretty much anything. She was faster, stronger, and smarter than us boys. I used to laugh as a kid because if you messed with me, my sister would beat you up! For some of you reading this, you might have experienced Shannon picking you up over her shoulders and throwing you on the ground. What makes me smile even more is that she still does this to people. If you look at her, you would never think she could do this. She is a beautiful petite woman that doesn't appear to have any meat on her bones. All I can say is never assume!

What a role reversal it was—my little brothers were now watching over me, longing to see me get up. They missed our harmless scuffles, and they knew that only God could bring me back. And they were battling for me in prayer. In writing his post, Dan appealed to all of the readers to join in the fight.

CaringBridge® Blog
She has a soft heart and tough skin. Shannon truly cares about people. Shannon would be praying for you and your family right now if you were in her shoes. Regardless if she knew you or not. That's just who she is.

It was bittersweet for my parents to have their family so united and yet to be going through such distress. My mother noted another incident that fueled the sense of hope that God was at work in the midst of our disaster. This time it was my brothers who were the recipients of an encouraging message.

> **Mom's Journal**
> Dan and Tim were in the elevator, and a nurse that had been with Shannon got in the elevator and asked them if they were Kerr McCauley. Then she said something was happening in Shannon's room, and she knew she was going to be OK.

The nurse was in tears, moved by a strong conviction that something unique was happening in my room, prompting her to think that I would be healed. My brothers knew that this something was God. That same day, my cousin's wife, Liz Matson, in North Carolina was praying, crying out to God later that night. Their teenage daughter came into the room where Liz was wrestling in prayer and said, "She's going to be OK." The faith of a child and the confident observation of a nurse helped to raise the spirits of my family in the thick of the crisis.

Jason and my father again took turns staying by my bedside that night, while my mother and Karen Hedstrom stayed at Kristi's apartment near the hospital. Stepping away from the hospital for the first time was heart-wrenching for my mother. Her journal tracked the distance and clocked the time, which felt far and long.

> **Mom's Journal**
> Even though it is only two blocks away, it was so hard to leave. I left at 9:30 p.m. and was back by 7:00 a.m.

Another morning dawned, but nothing had changed. The neurosurgeon detected no increased brain activity in the misty cloud of my coma, and my limbs didn't budge.

What also hadn't changed were the fervent prayers of my family and friends, near my hospital bed and farther away. They heard the doctors, and they listened to what God had to say about the whole situation.

Mom's Journal

I was praying with Jason in the walkway between the two wings, and God gave me the words to the song: "Whose report do you believe? We believe the report of the Lord!" And that is what we are doing.

God brought that song by Ron Kenoly to my mother's mind at just the right moment. "Whose Report Shall You Believe?" declares it like this:

Whose report
Will you believe?
We shall believe
The report of the Lord.
His report says
I am healed,
His report says
I am filled,
His report says
I am free,
His report says victory!
Are you healed?
Yes!
Are you filled?

Yes!

Have you got the victory?

Yes!

We would need to remember that strong message of victory as the doctors' reports kept presenting my family with a prognosis that spoke of defeat. From a medical standpoint, I really was unresponsive. The vigil continued.

At about 11:45 a.m., the doctors removed Kyra's ventilator, reducing her sedation medication so that her body could react to the procedure. Success—Kyra coughed and began moving! Jason looked on, and Kyra even spoke a word or two. Her vital signs were good, and the medical staff monitored her progress, watching for more indications that her brain was healing.

Because Kyra was still fragile while coming out of the induced coma, and because I was in such a severe state of brain injury, the hospital restricted the policy for visitors. We had such a constant flux of friends that the doctors were concerned about overstimulation. Loud sounds and stimuli triggered a rise in blood pressure, and we were too frail to handle all of the activity. So they insisted that no more than two visitors could come into each of our rooms at a time, and no children.

This didn't stop the flow of prayer, though, and Jason was so grateful. Kristi shared his thoughts in the CaringBridge® post that day:

CaringBridge® Blog

Jason has a message for you all: "Tell them I am humbled by the outpouring of prayers for my family. Thank them for their obedience to pray on behalf of the Kerrs. Let them know that our faith is unshakable in Jesus our Savior and King. May His name be lifted high. We are His faithful servants in good times and bad. To Him be the glory. As the Lord brings my family to mind, pray for Shannon's and Kyra's brains to be healed and made new."

My friend Brandy Jacobson, who visited me frequently, was one of the many who prayed. On Thursday, she had a vision of me talking to a crowd of women. This was not the first indication that I would eventually be healed—and telling about it—and her vision wouldn't be the last.

My brother Dan's wife, Beth, called my mother, telling her that God had reminded her of something that had taken place earlier in the year. On Memorial Day weekend, my brother Mike's father-in-law, Mike Ramsey, had spoken a word from God to me. He had said, "Shannon, don't be afraid!" I am generally a fearless person, so his simple statement had struck me as being unusual. *Afraid of what?* If God says to go left, I go left, and if He says to go right, I go right. No fear. It hadn't really made sense to me at the time. Now Beth and my mother were realizing that it was a message that applied to the current crisis.

> **Mom's Journal**
> We were thinking it was for now, and He wanted her to know He was going to bring her through this. Praise God! Just taking turns being in with her, I can feel You strong, Lord! Pat is spending most of his time with his baby girl.

My mother and Karen spent the night at Kristi's apartment again. It was so hard for everyone to see me like this, but it was also so hard to step away and not be looking.

Going back to the hospital the next morning, my mother agonized over the prospect of another anxious day of watching and waiting. The nightmare was encroaching on the nights and the days, all week long. She longed to speed up the pace of the healing process, to have her daughter back again.

> **Mom's Journal**
> I was walking into the hospital, and Karen and I passed two women. One woman said, "God wants you where He puts you, not where you want to be!"

My mother spontaneously turned her head toward the woman's assertive voice, focusing on what she had just heard. *Yes,* my mother thought, *this is where we are, and God is with us.* She had no doubt that God had put us here, and that was enough to enable her to step into another day of this crisis of uncertainty.

The crisis was mine, but I was unaware of it. While my family was enduring restless nights where deep sleep seemed to be a long-lost luxury, I was sleeping through everything. Darkness and dawn were all the same, and neither the stars nor the sunshine made a difference to my empty panorama. Day after day, night after night, I had no dramatic enlightenment, no divine visions—only oblivion. Now, on this side of that awful slumber, my family has been filling in the gaps of what happened while I was sleeping. They tell me about their sleeplessness and their struggle. As if waiting for me to wake up wasn't hard enough, they also faced hard decisions about how to proceed with my medical care. Friday was a day when they would have to choose what to do. Thankfully, God was with us here, too.

Jason woke up Friday morning in the small, sunless room, the concrete bunker that my family had occupied during this battle for my life, with a strange lump in the back of his throat. It didn't feel like a typical sore throat, but it was something he couldn't ignore. What bothered him more than the soreness was the realization that, with any kind of infection, he wouldn't be allowed to stand by my bedside or Kyra's, supporting us as we wrestled to recover from our injuries. As Jason would put it, he's not one to just pop pills to make the sun come out, but he was conflicted. This was no day to be getting sick.

When my mother arrived at the hospital, still remembering the woman's encouraging statement that God wanted her to be in this place, Jason told her about the ache in his throat. My mother's upbeat attitude and her faith in God's care were under attack, but her resolve didn't dwindle. She gently insisted that Jason should go to the ER in that same building and maybe get some medication. My father went along with him.

Jason only goes to the doctor if I sign him up for it. So there he was, an athletic, thirty-eight-year-old man, with his mother-in-law telling him to go to the ER and his father-in-law escorting him downstairs. It was the first time since Monday that Jason and my father had left the ICU together.

Before long, a doctor was available to see Jason, and my father accompanied him into the room. The doctor looked at Jason's throat and promptly determined the problem. Jason doesn't even remember what she said had caused the soreness. "It's not contagious," she said, giving him a pill. "You should be better in the next couple of hours."

At this, my quick-witted father said to the doctor, "Can you give him a shot?" Give him a shot? Jason doesn't like needles! I love hearing them tell this story of what was happening downstairs while I was sleeping. "We can't leave until we get something more than a pill," my father said, making the doctor laugh. But since the pill really was all that he needed, Jason managed to get out of there without anything else. I'm sure that she gave him the right pill, but the laughter was also good medicine.

The laughter almost felt odd to them, like an extinct species of life, a life from the past. As Jason now describes it, the hospital hallways were a walk through death and despair. Walking back in the direction of the ICU meant passing dozens of other rooms where hopelessness and death hung in the gaping doorways. Every step was draining. As he returned to face another day of heartbreaking vigil, Jason was thinking, *My issue is going to be OK, and I can go back again to sitting at the bedside of this situation.* The pill would take care of his sore throat, but there was a lump of anxiety that wouldn't disappear so quickly.

Jason and my father stepped into the elevator, joining four or five other people. Jason was in no mood for small talk, but my father commented on the weather. They hadn't even been outside since that cloudless Monday morning, and Jason was quiet, lost in the fog of his own thoughts. The elevator stopped at the fourth floor, then the fifth, and people were getting off.

"Are you OK?" a man in the elevator said to Jason as the doors closed again and they rose past the fifth floor. Head down, Jason looked to the side and noticed the kindly inquisitive face of a tall African man standing next to him. The man was slightly stooped, grasping the handles of a wheelchair where his mother sat. Both were wearing traditional African clothing, the vibrant fabrics even more vivid against the gray panels that encased the elevator.

Jason had nothing to say. Pat spoke up, saying, "Well, my daughter is fighting for her life." The elevator reached the seventh floor, where they would be getting off to join me and watch what appeared to be an endless fight yet again.

As the doors opened, the man also began to get off, pushing the wheelchair across the threshold and rolling into the open space between the four elevators. Turning toward Jason and my father, he said, "Can I pray for you?"

"Absolutely," Jason replied, now looking intently into the eyes of this man who had paused to pose the only question that mattered to him. The man's mother sat quietly in the wheelchair, not speaking any English.

The man began to pray, boldly proclaiming his faith that God would heal me. To Jason and my father, it was as if the skies of heaven had opened in that stark, sterile hospital hallway, and a flood of emotion and faith poured over them. Jason was filled with joy because of the obedience of the man to stop and pray in that moment. It would have been easy for any stranger to hear about our crisis and brush the conversation aside, casually saying that he would be praying for my family in some vague future tense.

Right through the final amen, it was a powerful prayer. Finishing, the man turned his eyes toward Jason and my father, addressing them with an earnestness that gripped their hearts. "Don't believe what they are telling you," he said, pointing down the hall toward the hospital wing where I was under the careful scrutiny of the doctors. "Believe what He tells you," he said, gesturing upward toward God in heaven. "She will be healed."

That declaration brought joy to Jason's spirit, invigorating him more than the pill he had swallowed downstairs. Now it was his turn for small talk. Jason asked the man, "Where are you from?"

"Swaziland," he answered. It had been exactly one year, to the day, since Jason and I had gone to Swaziland! Jason immediately felt the connection and mentioned that he had been there. The man didn't go into any detail though, and kept trying gently to redirect the conversation, not really saying much more.

Before pulling away to go see Kyra and me, Jason asked the man, "Can I pray for you?" The man chuckled, nothing more.

Only later did Jason realize how unusual the entire interaction had been. He never again saw the man from Swaziland, nor his sweet-tempered mother, although they had gotten off the elevator on the same floor. Our rooms were at the end of the hallway, and Jason became familiar with the faces of other patients and visitors as he walked back and forth. The man who had proclaimed a message of healing never reappeared. And he had acted as if he didn't need prayer. Could he have been an angelic messenger? If so, he wasn't the first angel to show up on the scene, nor the last.

We don't know exactly who he was, but we do know that what the delightfully intriguing man from Swaziland said about healing was exactly what my family needed to hear. Within a few hours they would be hearing something entirely different from the doctors.

My vital signs had remained steady overnight, but there had been no improvement in my brain activity. Lying feebly in the hospital bed all week was starting to take its toll on my limbs, so a physical therapist put boots on my feet to keep them in a flat position. This would prevent my Achilles tendon from tightening, although no one expected me to be running again anytime soon. What they expected was much worse.

Five doctors entered my room Friday morning and talked with Jason. Their tone seemed nonchalant to him as they spoke about what needed to happen next. "We have to take your wife off the ventilator," they said, explaining that there was a limit to how long I could rely on the equipment that was delivering oxygen to my dormant lungs. After removing the ventilator, they could perform a tracheostomy, they told him.

It was a hopeless situation, though. Signing the paperwork for the tracheostomy procedure was like authorizing nothing more than a desperate attempt to keep a vegetable alive. One of the neurosurgeons said, "The best-case scenario is that your wife will stare at a wall." Jason sensed the severity of my prognosis, while at the same time not really letting the bad reports rattle his core. If the tracheostomy could be a passageway for healing, then he wanted to open that channel. He signed the paper.

"I never saw Jason's faith waver," our friend Justin Mack later told us. "With one bad report after another, he didn't flinch." I know it was hard for Jason and for my whole family not only to see me in a coma but also to choose how to proceed with my treatment.

Justin noticed that whenever the doctors would approach Jason with another medical report, he would always respond calmly. After each doctor finished presenting the facts, Jason would say, "If you believe in Jesus, would you pray that He would heal my wife?" From what Justin observed, no one was offended by it. Jason wasn't oblivious to the medical reality, but he was aware of a larger reality in the hands of the Creator of the universe.

And there was evidence that the Creator was still at work. God, who gives life and breath to His creatures, was already demonstrating His power in Kyra. Her first full day off the ventilator went smoothly. The nurses kept her medicated to ease the pain from her injuries, but Kyra was increasingly responsive to stimuli around her. My mother was there to see her progress.

Mom's Journal
A nurse was doing something to her nose, and she said, "Ouch!" and hit her hand away. Love it! She hates the feeding tube in her nose. I think it itches. She will grab it and kind of pull on it. We have to keep telling her it's OK and move her hands. It is such a blessing to be able to sit here and just see the improvement in her.

It was also very special for both grandmothers to be at the hospital when Kyra had her first bath since the accident. Together, my mother and my mother-in-law slowly, tenderly combed the snarls out of Kyra's hair. A nurse then came and braided her hair, a touch of girlish beauty for a little seven-year-old princess who had endured a tangled, ugly wreck.

Meanwhile, the day plodded along, and Jason stayed close by my bedside, wistfully remembering that we had planned to go out on Friday night. We had talked about it on Sunday. Our church was producing a music album, and the recording would be a live event, an experience open to the public. We wanted to go, to sing in the crowd as part of River Valley Worship and tune our souls in praise to God.

But by Friday night, everything looked different than we had anticipated. Jason and I were now standing on the edge of heaven, just like the title of the album, but not as we had wished. Jason's place was with me, at Hennepin County Medical Center, where the line between earth and heaven was looking fuzzy. He wanted to stay by my side, on the edge of the chasm that gaped in front of us.

Friends from church, however, kept visiting the hospital that day and mentioning the upcoming event. They prodded Jason to consider going, advising him that a night of worshipping God in the church community would be a balm to his soul, a break from the harsh confines of the depressing hospital.

I don't know, Jason thought. *I don't need any questions. I don't need anything.*

"Come late," Justin Mack told him, suggesting that Jason could arrive subtly so that he could worship God without attracting a lot of attention personally. "We'll bring you in through the side door."

Jason decided to go, his desire to worship God winning out over his reluctance to join a crowd of onlookers. As night fell, his emotions were raw, having watched my status decline throughout the day. As he entered the auditorium, pastor and singer Ryan Williams was speaking on the platform and noticed Jason take a seat. Ryan began talking about a tragedy that had occurred in the community.

"I feel led to call out a deacon of ours, a young family with two young daughters," Ryan said. Most of the congregation was already somewhat aware of what had happened to us. Jason stayed where he was as Ryan began to pray for our family and then launched into the next song.

It was a new song that we had learned recently in church, and we had sung it a lot in the previous weeks. I had probably sung it, too, the Sunday before the accident. The lyrics to "I Am Healed" were incredibly appropriate, as desperation and faith intersected on Friday night.

Lord, I'm desperate for Your power,
I need a miracle.
Lord, I'm desperate for Your touch,
I need a miracle.

Heaven's floor is shaking,
Healing rain is falling.
Heaven's floor is shaking,
Healing rain is falling.

I am healed, I know I am,
For my God says I am.
Come what may, my faith will stand.
I am healed, I know I am.

You are speaking, faith is rising,
I need a miracle.
Christ my Healer, the work is done:
I have my miracle.

Sickness, you have no power here,
Darkness, you have no power here,
Chaos, you have no power here,
In Jesus' Name.

Jason dropped to his knees, praying, and in that moment, he decided. *That's what I'm believing.* Worshipping God replenished his soul, and he had no doubt that those lyrics were for me. I would be healed.

While Jason's faith was soaring with the music, something much more sobering was happening at the hospital. My father, Ben Markham, and Kristi Hedstrom were gathered at my bedside that night, and the doctors came into the room with huge clamps. They applied the scissor-like clamps to my toes and fingers, watching for any reaction from my body.

There was no response, no wincing, no "Ow!" They concluded that there was no sign of brain activity. The axons in my brain stem were shredded, they assessed, and axons in adults don't regenerate. The room was dark and quiet as the doctors examined my status, beginning to question whether or not it would even be worthwhile to perform the tracheostomy that Jason had approved. My body was still bloody, too fragile for the nurses to clean, too fragile for much of anything. All week long, Jason had been directing the doctors' attention to the photograph from the swing dance, saying, "I'm going to dance with her next year." Now the doctors weren't sure if I would even be alive, much less dance.

To state it bluntly, the doctors thought it was time to pull the plug. As Kristi recalls, the doctors told the three of them, "If you don't remove the ventilator, and if you proceed with the tracheostomy, then you're basically looking at starvation and dehydration issues." Kristi grappled with what that meant. She realized that the doctors were actually saying that they expected me to die, and that it would be better to let me die naturally rather than prolong a situation that would not end well later. If they didn't pull the plug, I would become a vegetable. Eventually they would have to withdraw the flow of nutrients, and my body would then perish.

The dark room got darker as the doctors left the room. The news was too heavy to bear, and my father, Ben, and Kristi felt as if their hopes of healing from heaven had been beaten down to the ground. Kristi remembers that they didn't know how to process this harsh diagnosis, so instead they stopped thinking and just prayed.

They were sitting by my bed, holding the burden of the devastating news, when Jason returned from the album recording. "Oh! You should've been there!" he said to them, looking at the bleak scene as he stepped closer. "God is in control. Shannon will be healed."

Ben later described the peace and joy and life that penetrated the hospital room when Jason spoke into the hopelessly dark silence. "He was glowing," Ben said, "like Moses when he came down from the mountain after speaking with God." My condition had not changed—not yet—but Jason was confident.

Jason listened closely to their account of the doctors' advice and then firmly stated that he would not pull the plug. "I heard from the Lord," he said. "You heard from doctors. I will not pull the plug."

Ben watched as my father instantly stood up, hugged Jason, and said, "Thank you. I needed to hear that." Jason insisted that my parents go home and get a good night's sleep. Exhausted, my father whispered good night to me, overwhelmingly relieved that he was only saying good night to his daughter—not goodbye.

Jason remained by my side throughout the night, while his parents stayed close to Kyra, watching their bruised granddaughter sleep in a room filled with stuffed animals and balloons. The cheerful gifts that surrounded them seemed peculiar in the face of so much pain.

At 10:00 p.m., my father went down the same elevator where earlier that day he and Jason had received a message of hope, delivered passionately by the enigmatic man from Swaziland. Now it was Jason who was the messenger of hope, more determined than ever that I would be healed.

Tired from watching me sleep for five days but trusting that God was in all of this, my father found my mother waiting downstairs. "I have to get out of here," he told her. She sensed that he was carrying a burden as they drove from downtown Minneapolis to Owatonna, their first trip home since they had dashed out the door on Monday morning.

"You don't know what I know," my father told her, his voice more serious than usual. "You don't know what I've heard."

My mother wanted to hear all of it and listened as he filled her in on the tumultuous details, starting with the doctors' recommendation to pull the plug. "I know what God is speaking to us," she said to my father, reminding him of the promises that God had made. "God wouldn't have sent that angel today to tell you that Shannon is going to be OK if He was going to take her away." My mother, just as weary as my father was, told him that they had to stand on God's promises and go forward. He agreed. They were in this together as my parents, and they were united in their faith.

They reached Owatonna at 11:15 p.m., their eyes heavy but their spirits lifted by their faith. Before turning out the light by the bed, my mother opened a devotional book and began to read. She almost leapt out of bed when she reached these words: "'For my thoughts are not your thoughts, neither are your ways my ways,' declares the LORD" (Isaiah 55:8).

"Pat!" she exclaimed. "He is telling us again that it doesn't matter what the doctors said. He told us this morning, and He is telling us now. His ways are His ways, and they are not our ways."

Her journal entry ended with a small exclamation point that said a lot. It was a sentence of gratitude, with a hint of healing.

Mom's Journal
Lord, thank You for keeping our girls safe!

On Saturday morning from 8:00 a.m. to 9:30 a.m., dozens of people in the area gathered to pray for Kyra and me. Our own church community, the Apple Valley campus of River Valley Church, north of our home in Lakeville, hosted one of the prayer meetings, opening the auditorium for people to come and go informally. On the west side of Minneapolis, others congregated at the Shakopee campus, while the same was happening further south, in my childhood hometown of Owatonna.

Because Kristi was posting minimal details on the CaringBridge® website, to protect our family from the well-meaning curiosity of outside observers and to prevent the spread of alarming rumors, most of the people didn't know how delicately my life was wavering. She hadn't announced anything about the difficult decisions that had transpired the previous day. The prospect of pulling the plug was never written in print. Instead, Kristi had appealed for prayer, just as Jason had requested. Keep praying, she said:

CaringBridge® Blog
- For the swelling in Shannon's brain to completely dissipate.
- For Shannon to move and respond to the doctors' tests—pray for miraculous progress.
- For Kyra's brain and other injuries to heal quickly, and for her physical comfort in the meantime.
- For wisdom for the team of dedicated doctors treating Shannon and Kyra.
- For spiritual protection and childlike faith for each person who is praying for the Kerr family, and for the spiritual endurance to continue.

Jason stepped away from the hospital to huddle with our

friends in prayer at the Apple Valley campus, along with his mother and his younger sister, Michelle. My family was greatly encouraged by the many believers who rose to the challenge of standing in the gap on our behalf, praying with strength when we were debilitated. Those who prayed were on the front lines in a spiritual battle, resisting the destructive thoughts of the enemy and trusting that God would be victorious. The physical injuries from the accident were part of a larger spiritual war between death and life. And they knew that God, the giver of life, is the only one who can heal.

My father-in-law, Terry, maintained the vigil at the hospital. Each morning at about 7:00 a.m., a team of five or six doctors would stop and talk with him as they made their rounds to evaluate the patients. On Saturday morning, one of the neurosurgeons entered Kyra's room, having just checked on me.

"How is Shannon?" Terry asked the doctor.

"Are you Jason's father?" she replied, and he nodded. With tears in her eyes, the neurosurgeon asked Terry to step into the hallway. "I don't think your son is understanding what is going to happen," she said. "He needs to prepare his children for the fact that Shannon isn't going to make it."

Terry didn't know what to do with that information. He had never had a bad experience with a doctor and had no reason to doubt their assessment. Recognizing that the doctors were exercising their profession to the best of their ability, Terry was praying for them. He knew that God was in control of the situation, including the doctors, and he also knew that God could heal.

We are praying for healing, Terry thought. *But is God going to heal?* Since he had been focusing on caring for Kyra, he hadn't heard about the unusual events on Friday—the man from Swaziland who had declared that I would be healed, and the song at the album recording that had reinforced that same message. Believing that God could heal was one thing, but stating outright that He would definitely heal me was something else. Terry was trusting and praying, just like everyone else, but he was afraid to be so bold. And now he had the tough job of telling Jason what the neurosurgeon had said.

Before Jason returned from the prayer meeting, my parents arrived at the hospital. My mother had called Aunt Peggy on the drive from Owatonna, and their conversation was filled with encouragement. Aunt Peggy told her that she had prayed for two hours on Friday night and that it was a very powerful moment. She had felt God saying, "I gave you the power and authority to move the mountain. Use that authority!" My mother knew that with faith in God, they could see mountains move, and she was ready to see my vaporous coma blow away in the winds of faith.

My mother walked into Kyra's room and began talking with Jason's older sister, Marcie, who had stayed overnight in the hospital. During the night, her sleepy niece had asked for a drink of water, and that small request was a big sign that Kyra was gradually reviving from her heavily medicated condition.

The devastating information that was weighing on Terry after his conversation with the neurosurgeon became secondary as he watched his precious granddaughter slowly getting better. He started to tell my mother and Jason about the doctor's warning, but they didn't really want to hear the negative report. There was no disrespect of the doctors' medical opinions. What prevailed was Jason's perspective that God's report was the only one that mattered. Jason and my parents were choosing to believe that Jesus would restore me, and Terry and Kristine willingly watched to see what God would do. The doctors were now tasked with determining when my body would be ready for the tracheostomy, which Jason had endorsed and entrusted to God.

Most of my family was clustered around Kyra, absorbed in the suspense of her progress. My mother jotted in her journal what it was like, observing Kyra throughout the day.

Mom's Journal

I have been sitting all day with her. The tube for feeding her and the oxygen mask make her crazy. She sat up in bed with her eyes open and then she lay back down again. This afternoon she was a bit uncomfortable, and they said, "Kyra, what is wrong?" She said, "My bottom hurt, and my tummy hurt." So even though we don't want you to hurt, we are glad you are telling us that. She is definitely waking up more and more. They just took an IV port out of her hand, and she cried out, "Ouch!" It's all so positive.

In the early afternoon, the doctors came to wake up Kyra completely. Until that point, she was still medicated to buffer the effects of her injuries. About ten doctors stood outside her room, waiting to see what would happen when she woke up. Her skull had been fractured in the impact of the collision, and there was no way to predict whether she had suffered long-term damage.

Terry was a witness to that pivotal moment. Jason had said to him beforehand, "Dad, when she is brought out of the coma, I want her to recognize somebody." No one knew if she would.

It had been a while since Kyra had seen her grandparents from Michigan, and Terry had grown a goatee in the meantime. "I've got to shave this off because she has never seen me in a goatee," he said to Jason, half-jokingly. As he went into her hospital room, though, his appearance was the least of his concerns. Terry was both eager and fearful to look at his granddaughter, wondering if she would really be OK.

A crowd of strange faces peered at her, as doctors and nurses surrounded their young patient. They administered the treatment to pull Kyra out of the induced coma and sat her up in bed. The buzzing equipment in the hospital room was an odd soundtrack to the emotional event.

Then Kyra looked over, saw Terry, and said, "Hi, Grandpa, thanks for coming!" It was miraculous. She was awake, and she was thinking. She could even remember that her grandparents lived far away, and her simple expression of gratitude for her grandfather's presence was the most amazing sentence he had heard in a long time.

"What is your doggie's name?" Terry asked her, his voice warm and quivering with emotion.

"Moe," Kyra answered.

It was a wonderful moment. Kyra was miraculously alive! Other than the twisted metal wreckage of our van, there had been nothing between her body and the semitrailer truck that had crashed into us at 60 mph. God had shielded her, and she had survived. At first, she was a little confused about what had actually happened, seemingly unaware of the accident. The last thing she remembered was falling on the broken glass bowl in the kitchen on Sunday night. Little Jaydalin stood by Kyra's bedside saying, "But we were in a car."

Kyra and Jaydalin

Soon my family would be learning more about who was in that car. It was Saturday afternoon, and the miraculous story was only starting to unfold. For now, the recovery process was happening one hour at a time. Kyra was still very sore, a broken collarbone and two cracks in her pelvic bone keeping her in bed. But at least she was awake, and my family was relieved, rejoicing in God's care.

Mom's Journal

Kyra is really starting to look like Kyra Jo again. Can't stop praising God for what He is doing and the miracle of her life!

I'm sure it was captivating to watch Kyra, to look into her sparkling eyes and catch a glimpse of the little girl we love, whose life had been spared. It was natural for visitors to want to be in the pediatric unit. Going to visit me was a much harder experience. Even the environment around my hospital room was unwelcoming. Across the hall was a city gang member who had been shot, and police officers were guarding the area while gang members came and went to visit the wounded man. Sometimes tempers flared as arguments broke out among the visitors. The lurid noise in the hallway was a sharp contrast to the sobering quietness of my ongoing coma.

Jason and the rest of my family didn't give up, and they kept asking people to pray. As Kristi posted on CaringBridge® that afternoon, there is power in the Word of God, and she passed along Jason's request. He wanted everyone to read, believe, and pray through three specific Bible passages on behalf of Kyra and me. Kristi quoted them fully on the website.

> The LORD is my strength and my defense;
>   he has become my salvation.
> Shouts of joy and victory
>   resound in the tents of the righteous:
> "The LORD's right hand has done mighty things!
> The LORD's right hand is lifted high;
>   the LORD's right hand has done mighty things!"
> **I will not die but live,**
>   **and will proclaim what the LORD has done.**
> (Psalm 118:14–17, emphasis added)

Kristi typed the last two lines in boldface, affirming the conviction that I would not die but live. The next passage was Psalm 91.

> Whoever dwells in the shelter of the Most High
>   will rest in the shadow of the Almighty.
> I will say of the LORD, "He is my refuge and my fortress,
>   my God, in whom I trust."

Surely he will save you
    from the fowler's snare
    and from the deadly pestilence.
He will cover you with feathers,
    and under his wings you will find refuge;
    his faithfulness will be your shield and rampart.
You will not fear the terror of night,
    nor the arrow that flies by day,
nor the pestilence that stalks in the darkness,
    nor the plague that destroys at midday.
A thousand may fall at your side,
    ten thousand at your right hand,
    but it will not come near you.
You will only observe with your eyes
    and see the punishment of the wicked.

If you say, "The LORD is my refuge,"
    and you make the Most High your dwelling,
no harm will overtake you,
    no disaster will come near your tent.
For he will command his angels concerning you
    to guard you in all your ways;
they will lift you up in their hands,
    so that you will not strike your foot against a stone.
You will tread on the lion and the cobra;
    you will trample the great lion and the serpent.

"Because he loves me," says the LORD, "I will rescue him;
    I will protect him, for he acknowledges my name.
He will call on me, and I will answer him;
    I will be with him in trouble,
    I will deliver him and honor him.
With long life I will satisfy him
    and show him my salvation."

Jason picked that passage with conviction and eyes of untiring faith, seeing in these words an abundance of powerful promises. Looking at those verses again now, we see that angels had been part of the picture all along. Only later would we learn more about the angelic presence that surrounded the story.

The third passage was an account of healing, taken from the Gospels. Earlier that day, my mother had been talking with Mike Ramsey, telling him about Aunt Peggy's experience in prayer. They were agreeing that with faith in God, mountains can move. Mike told my mother that he had been reading the Gospel of Matthew that morning and that he, too, had been reminded that Jesus gave His disciples authority to heal the sick. Jason's choice of Matthew 8:5-10 echoed that same faith.

> *When Jesus had entered Capernaum, a centurion came to him, asking for help. "Lord," he said, "my servant lies at home paralyzed, suffering terribly."*
>
> *Jesus said to him, "Shall I come and heal him?"*
>
> *The centurion replied, "Lord, I do not deserve to have you come under my roof. But just say the word, and my servant will be healed. For I myself am a man under authority, with soldiers under me. I tell this one, 'Go,' and he goes; and that one, 'Come,' and he comes. I say to my servant, 'Do this,' and he does it."*
>
> *When Jesus heard this, he was amazed and said to those following him, "Truly I tell you, I have not found anyone in Israel with such great faith."*

The great faith of my friends was at work while they prayed for me from afar. The same was happening in my hospital room. My family asked for no visitors on Saturday and Sunday, wanting to see if silence and the absence of stimuli would help reduce the swelling in my brain and enable my body to rest. But the momentum did not wane, as the day that had begun with church prayer meetings all over the area continued with prayer in the privacy of the ICU. My father had hung Scripture verses on the wall in my room, and my family prayed out loud, into the night.

At 2:00 a.m. my father and Jason were worshipping God together, their hands lifted into the air. They were talking and praising God, with worship music playing in the background. A nurse came into the room and with displeasure said, "Really? It's two in the morning." They didn't even know what time it was.

"You really have to tone it down because it's too loud," she said. They reduced their volume, but the sincerity of that moment of raw worship didn't diminish at all. Together, my whole family was genuinely worshipping God, regardless of how dim the circumstances were. My mother's journal that night shared the same sentiment.

Mom's Journal

My baby girl Shannon is resting in God's hands, and she is going to start opening her eyes soon. Praise You, Lord, for Your healing power. We trust in You completely!

Kyra was not only awake, she was also very alert. That was reason for rejoicing, and Jason was elated. She recognized all four of her grandparents, which was incredibly heartwarming. Kristi's post that day was happily titled: *Hello Kyra!*

Now Kyra could see the notes that people had written to her in erasable marker on a whiteboard in her hospital room. Kristi had written in bright red, "You are such a brave girl! Love you so much!" Kyra's middle name is Jolee, and many of us endearingly call her Jo Jo. Her sweet nickname was all over that whiteboard.

Others had sent pictures, including her second-grade class at school. Sixteen of her classmates had each drawn a colorful heart on construction paper and posed individually for a picture. They made a poster with all of the photos, plus one photo of the whole group, and across the top printed their most important message: "We are praying for you, Kyra!"

Kyra wasn't ready to go back to school yet, but her childlike energy was starting to return. Out of the blue, Kyra asked if she could watch the movie *Alvin and the Chipmunks*. She was able to eat and drink a little bit, although she still had a feeding tube. The doctors removed her catheter, and the fluid in her lungs was clearing. So far her progress was exceeding expectations, and everyone hoped that this would continue.

The hours in my room were significantly darker and quieter. I wasn't overtly declining, but I also wasn't showing any dramatic signs of improvement. The doctors were evaluating when they could perform an MRI, once the swelling on my brain had reduced enough for the examination to be effective.

So my family waited, worshipping God amid the swirling uncertainty of my medical condition. My mother penned her thoughts briefly, praising God and jotting something similar to the lyrics of Karen Wheaton's song "Look What the Lord Has Done." This had become the mantra of her faith.

Mom's Journal

Look what the Lord has done
He healed my body
He touched my mind
He saved me just in time
I will praise Your name!!

She added two exclamation points.

The following morning was not easy, though. Jason asked people to fast and pray on Monday, the day that marked one week since the accident. While I hovered between life and death in intensive care, he knew that we needed intensive prayer. My mother, who still held strongly to her faith that God was doing amazing things, wrote some sobering words in her journal.

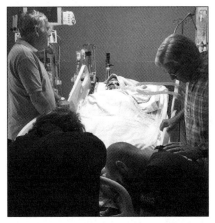

Jason, Dad, Mom, Pastor Greg praying at bedside

Mom's Journal

Went down to your room this morning, Shannon. It's super hard for me to see you like this. It kills my mother's heart. Dad and I prayed with the authority God gives us for healing. But the Lord let me see a lot of A's coming up on the vent, which said that you are assisting with your breaths. Can't believe we have been in this a week already.

This was now the second Monday in a row that would not be a normal workday. Jason's routine was stripped away from him as he stepped away from his job responsibilities at Jimmy John's for days that turned into weeks. "I could only focus on my kids and my wife," Jason said. Delegating the overseeing of the restaurants was difficult. Since it was September, the staff was transitioning, with college and high school students going back to their class schedules. But Jason had no doubt that watching over his family was his biggest priority.

At the corporate level, Jimmy John's pitched in to supply maintenance technicians and equipment, as well as coaches to help the local managers. It was a burst of help, easing a bit of the strain on Jason's shoulders as he carried the burden of our family crisis. Financially, the pause in our restaurant business hurt us pretty badly. There was no other choice because holding onto life itself was the only thing that mattered.

As the days wore on, Terry and Kristine were vital to keeping our busy household humming, as only grandparents can really do. They had flown into town from Michigan with only a duffle bag, not knowing how long the ordeal would last, so they went to Goodwill to get some clothes and eventually settled in for a while at our house. The constant companionship of visitors in our home was overwhelming, and yet the incredible outpouring of help from our church community touched them. "There was not a need that wasn't met," my mother-in-law said, reflecting on those early days.

As grandparents, Terry and Kristine were there not only receiving the gestures of friendship from our community but also nurturing the grandchildren. They had already developed a close connection to Trenton and Braylon during the period when we lived near them in Michigan, and they were glad to be present and spend more time with the girls. Now that Kristine was in the role of a substitute mother, she wasn't strict with the kids, but she was strict about how much food they had in their mouths at one time! Just like a good grandmother!

And Terry wanted to be there—to really be there—for our two boys. Since Jason was at the hospital so much, Terry hoped to assure Trenton and Braylon that they weren't lost in the shuffle.

Jason has a very hands-on approach to being a father, so the boys felt his absence. Terry understood. "It didn't matter what they wanted to do," Terry said. "If they wanted to go sit in the middle of the woods calling for coyotes and ask me questions, I was going to be the grandpa who was there for them." He did that so well.

It was good having Jaydalin at home, her playful outlook adding an extra spark of life at the house alongside her brothers. Three of the four tall stools at the kitchen counter were filled, and there was hope that Kyra would take her spot with her siblings soon. Trenton and Braylon hadn't been to the hospital since that first day, but as they continued with their schoolwork and sports activities, they enjoyed having their vibrant little sister back with them. This was the girl who could twirl like a little doll or cuddle one of the chickens in our backyard, her eyes beaming with sweet mischief.

Of course, the children knew how serious the situation was. They knew that the possibility of passing from earth to heaven is a reality, and that life and death are in the hands of God. At my prompting, they had just read the book *Heaven Is for Real* about a month before the accident. Todd Burpo's story about the near-death experience of his four-year-old son, Colton, had impressed upon them the wonders of heaven. And in August when we were on vacation, I was reading a book about a woman in a coma. The children had been intrigued by the story, asking me to read more to them while we were out fishing in a boat. God used these true stories to prepare our children for this crisis in a way that Jason and I could never have planned. The ideas of life and death and eternal life were familiar to them, and they were praying that God would uphold my life.

In addition to clinging to life by fasting privately that day, our friends also displayed their support publicly. A group of women in Owatonna called MOPS, mothers of preschoolers, organized a prayer walk around Hennepin County Medical Center. We didn't even know them personally. They announced it via social media and through the CaringBridge® site, asking people to meet at

7:15 p.m. on 8th Street in Minneapolis, across the street from the ER entrance. The plan was for everyone to wear a yellow shirt and bring either a yellow balloon or a candle, shining a bright light of faith at sunset.

It was a crowd! There were yellow shirts everywhere, all around the block. Some of them decorated their balloons by writing Bible verses on them, and one verse in particular became a theme for my family: "Ask and it will be given to you; seek and you will find; knock and the door will be opened to you" (Matthew 7:7).

Jason and my parents joined the prayerful parade on the city sidewalks, and at the end of the walk, the group gathered on a small plot of grass outside the hospital. Placing some candles on the ground in the shape of a heart, they stopped to pray together. Jason and my parents knelt on the grass, the flames from the candles flickering beneath their faces in the dusk, while everyone stood behind them. The crowd sang songs of praise, and their presence was very meaningful to my family. It was also impressive to the hospital staff, especially when the group said that they were praying not only for me but also for everyone else in the hospital. Usually a marching crowd like that is picketing against something, but in this case they were *for* something, instead. The sunny yellow ensemble radiated a peaceful message of faith in God, casting rays of hope as nighttime settled on the hospital.

Onlookers saw it, of course, but more importantly, God heard the prayers that many people lifted upward that day. Afterward, Jason asked Kristi to post this statement on CaringBridge®: "Thank you for fasting and praying. The Lord hears our cry."

That day, my friend Hannah Baldwin had a remarkable experience, confirming that God was indeed hearing. She lives in Wisconsin, and her three young children were sick at various times in those first several days. Because of this, she wasn't able to visit me in the hospital for quite a while. But she felt called to fight for me in prayer, from a distance. She had never prayed so much before in her life, and she found herself even praying in her sleep.

Hannah had a divine vision on Monday, a picture in her

mind of God touching my brain. She said that healing light was spreading over me. In the image that she saw, it was a gradual healing, whole and complete but not fast. With the vision, she was also struck by the words of a biblical prophet:

"Write down the revelation
    and make it plain on tablets
    so that a herald may run with it.
For the revelation awaits an appointed time;
    it speaks of the end
    and will not prove false.
Though it linger, wait for it;
    it will certainly come
    and will not delay"
(Habakkuk 2:2–3).

Hannah was certain that I would be healed, and she also knew that it would not happen quickly. It would require waiting on God's timing.

My parents went home to sleep that night to be refreshed for another day of waiting. As they went, they were praying for restoration for me, for every brain cell in my head. I kept sleeping.

The yellow balloons had floated high in the sky on Monday evening, and God had heard the prayers of the crowd under the darkening skies. The swelling in my brain was still significant, but as Tuesday dawned, I was ready for the tracheostomy. Even minimal, slow progress was better than the stagnancy that had become the norm within the past week.

The tracheostomy aimed to reduce the risk of respiratory infection and to surgically provide an alternative airway to ease the flow of oxygen, thus preparing my body for whatever phase of recovery might come next. With the swelling slightly reduced, medical personnel had performed an MRI on my brain. Our friend Greg Youmans, who is the Care Pastor of our church, was with my father when they delivered the MRI results. The doctors concluded that my brain was severely damaged—basically, a mess— and offered little hope of brain matter regeneration and renewal.

Greg listened to the doctors' grim update, bracing himself to comfort my family. Before he could respond, my father said, "Now we have documentation for a miracle." Sober and yet optimistic, my father was confident that the negative medical report would later confirm the dramatic healing work of God. At some point in the future, we would look back and see the contrast between massive brain damage and the curative power of the Almighty God. The MRI was not marking the end of my life, only the beginning of a miraculous awakening. The question was, when would I wake up, open my eyes, and be able to look at what God had done?

Every insight that God was granting to people indicated that my healing would not be immediate. The prayer channels kept flowing as my mother kept counting the days in her journal. On Tuesday, she welcomed one of our restaurant business associates who came to the hospital to plead to God on my behalf as part of the healing process.

Mom's Journal

Jim Lemond, who tiles our Jimmy John's stores, has the gift of healing. He and his sister came up, and we prayed over Shannon and Kyra. It is so awesome to pray for healing with the authority for healing that God has given us! Amen.

This was neither a fanatical prayer nor a religious fantasy, as some might say. Jim Lemond was not trying to create some magically powerful effect based on his own skill. It was a fervent prayer of faith, voiced by a man who set aside his tile-work craftsmanship for a few minutes in order to humbly kneel at the feet of God, who alone can do all things.

Apparently God was choosing to show through my weak, thin, and feeble body the magnificence of His strength—without hurrying. From a physical viewpoint, it was a long wait. Looking at it from God's perspective, there was no rush because everything was firmly, safely, in His control. The full demonstration of healing would come slowly, intentionally putting God at the center of attention as people continued to pray, urgently and earnestly. "The name of the LORD is a fortified tower; the righteous run to it and are safe" (Proverbs 18:10). If I was ever going to run again, it would come as the result of many people praying, running to the most secure place that exists—the name of God. The fortified tower of faith would be their stronghold while they watched me recover, and God would be my fortress as I lay within the confines of my bed. The prayers for my healing didn't produce an obvious result right away—I didn't jump out of bed—but each prayer was like one more yellow balloon, soaring upward to the skies. God saw each floating yellow balloon and heard each steady, unseen prayer, and He knew that we would see more miraculous surprises in upcoming days.

In the meantime, all was not gloomy darkness! There is nothing like the loving gaze of a son to brighten a room. Even better, two sons, side by side. On Tuesday, Jason brought Trenton and Braylon to the hospital to see Kyra and me. The boys hadn't been there since day one, when I had come out of emergency surgery, and they had yet to see their sister Kyra. They were her big brothers, but they were also very young to be facing the horrors of the accident. The trauma of even knowing about our injuries was bad enough, and Jason didn't want to aggravate the situation by overwhelming the boys too soon. But after that first week, the timing seemed right for them to visit.

Of course, just like when they had visited on day one, I was still in no condition to notice their expressions when Trenton and Braylon entered my room. Jason was initiating a new habit for them, going to see their comatose mother—their mom who didn't seem like mom. They visited regularly after that, observing my healing process along with the rest of the family. This gave them the opportunity to make sense of things firsthand and, eventually, to celebrate any breakthrough when the coma would turn into a glimpse of clarity.

Kyra, though, remembers well the feeling she had when Trenton and Braylon first came to see her. Looking back at the experience, she said, "I just felt loved." Their visit even moved her to joyful tears because she was so happy to have her big brothers with her. Her mind was a bit foggy, and she forgot how old her siblings were, thinking that each of them was one year younger. "Trenton, you're twelve, right?" Kyra said hesitantly.

"No, I'm thirteen," Trenton replied. But it didn't matter because Kyra's math skills returned soon after that. What did matter was that she was alive, and what prevailed in that moment was her love—and her victory smile.

Braylon wandered over to the side of the room and wrote in green marker on the whiteboard—first a smiley face, then a heart. Then he signed his name and printed these three big words: *I love you*. With the warm excitement of their visit still lingering in her mind, Kyra topped off the day with a few sips of a chocolate milkshake and finally got to watch her chosen movie, *Alvin and the Chipmunks*.

My children were surrounded by people who cared for them,

and they had Jason's constant, fatherly love. Things had changed, however, and my role as their active, able-bodied mother was suspended in my unpredicted slumber. But God wasn't done working. That same day, Tammy Gonzalez reached out to my mother with a message of hope. Tammy had babysat my brothers and me when we were children in Owatonna and has kept in contact with our family ever since.

Mom's Journal
Tammy Gonzalez sent me a devotion she was reading. Saying, trust Me. Refuse to worry for I am your strength and song and do not look at difficult times. Keep bringing our minds back to Him.

Tammy, the woman who had cared for me as a child, was now extending her care to my mother and to me in this moment when I was more vulnerable than ever. I was more helpless than a newborn child. My mother, my own babysitter Tammy, and I— we were all mothers now—each of us needed to do nothing more than keep trusting God, resting in His loving arms.

WEDNESDAY
September 23, 2015

April and Ben Markham had left town, returning to their home in Florida after their six-day visit. During that week, every time April stopped by my room in the hospital, she had seen the same angelic figure poised with strength at the head of my bed. The comforting presence of God was sustaining my beating heart, even though the coma continued to linger.

At first glance, more apparent to anyone walking into the room was a handwritten, black-marker sign on a piece of paper near my head. The alert read: *No Bone on L.* With the comings and goings of various medical staff, it was a well-placed warning that a portion of my skull was missing on the left side of my head, following the procedure that had eased the pressure as my brain swelled. The bandage above my left ear was also labeled: *No bone.* These notices would prevent harm so that no one would prod that spot unknowingly.

On Wednesday, in addition to those medical warning signs, the hospital gave me a customized helmet. This may sound like a

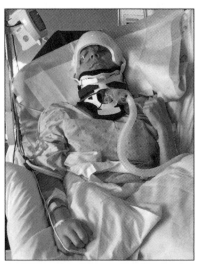

Shannon in coma, helmet, strapped to bed

regression, but it was progress! The doctors decided that moving me to a sitting position for two hours would help my lungs to heal and prevent bedsores from becoming a problem. The helmet protected my brain from any accidental jolting during the transition to an upright posture. The nurses vigilantly propped me up. With this change, the pressure in my brain skyrocketed to 30mmHG, which is dangerously high, given that intracranial hypertension levels above 20mmHG require immediate attention. They promptly addressed the concern and reduced the pressure to 17mmHG, closer to the normal range of 5 to 15mmHG. The helmet was a startling sight, but underneath it, my facial swelling and bruising had begun to decrease.

Sitting up for two hours was a milestone for me. My friend Stephanie Balvin came to the hospital that day and sat by my bedside with my father for twelve hours. Also, my friend Katie Moras came to sit near me on her lunch break from work. Their visits were a huge encouragement to my parents, their gestures of companionship demonstrating a commitment to friendship in all of life's silent shadows.

While I was consistently sleeping, Kyra, on the other hand, wasn't sleeping very much. The activity in her room was totally crazy, according to my mother, but in a good way. During her occupational therapy session, Kyra read part of a book in the Froggy series by Jonathan London and successfully completed an exercise where she pretended to go fishing for the letters of her name.

As Kyra's mind made strides, so did her injured body. Tests indicated that Kyra had some air in her chest cavity, so she was still receiving oxygen to allow the air in her chest cavity to dissipate. Freshly bathed, she dressed herself in her own pink pajamas and got a ride in a wheelchair down the hallway toward the pediatric unit, her first trip outside the boundaries of the ICU. The multicolor blanket tucked around her in the wheelchair paled in comparison with her sweet smile. Then, with a little help from Jason, she walked part of the way back to her room in the ICU, her broken pelvic bones already able to stabilize her small frame.

Another visit from her siblings was a highlight of the day for Kyra. Jaydalin brought her a stuffed Minnie Mouse doll, which she loved, and all four of them played a game together. My mother was there to watch the bond between her beloved grandchildren.

> **Mom's Journal**
> The kids came up to see Kyra. She just comes alive when they get here. Blesses all of us to watch. God is good. He is walking us through this. We just need you.

Her journal entry turned toward me in that last line, a plea for me to return to being the daughter that she knows. *We just need you.* It sounded desperate. That same day, my childhood babysitter again sent a message, thoughts of faith from one mother to another.

> **Mom's Journal**
> From Tammy Gonzalez's devotion. Wait quietly in your presence while My thoughts form silently in the depths of your being. We don't want to keep our heart earthbound. He is the creator of the universe but He chooses to make His home in our heart. It's there we know Him. Ask His Spirit to quiet my mind so I can hear God's small quiet voice. I am speaking to you continually: words of life, peace, love. Turn your heart to receive abundant blessing!

The thoughts that Tammy shared with my mother were scattered and yet they were solidly meaningful, reminding her to look not only at me, longing for the moment when I would awaken from the coma. There was more at stake than my body lying in bed —there was a thriving heart and mind and soul as well. Because when we look upward, turning our earthbound minds and hearts toward God, abundant blessing awaits us. God's words of life are what we really need as living beings. We look, and we see.

The seeing was about to begin. My mother wrote something on the last page of Wednesday's journal entry that seemed to be an afterthought at the end of the day. In retrospect, it's ironic that she mentioned it so briefly, when soon we would learn how significant it really was. It was the beginning of being awakened to what is perhaps the most extraordinary and miraculous episode in this entire story.

Mom's Journal

Steph was telling us that the man who got Jayda out of the car was the second person on the scene. Said that when he read the part in the paper about there being three people in the car, he said that was wrong. He said there were four. There was a lady front passenger seat that wasn't hurt, speaking to Shannon. He swears by it and what he saw. He wants to talk to Jason. It could only be an angel. Someone had to take the blow for Kyra. It's such a miracle that they are here and Kyra is awake!

As Wednesday ended, the day closed with the incessant shadows of my coma, and also with the fuzzy details of an astonishing eyewitness account from the scene of the accident. My mother had been counting the days of our crisis—it was day ten—but now she was counting how many people had been in the van during the crash. Were there three or four? The eager expectation of a conversation settled over the family as they restlessly tried to get some sleep. Not conscious of the excitement, I slept more than anyone, in the deep unconsciousness of my coma.

Night and day, beyond the hospital walls, beyond the time zone in Minneapolis, people were still praying. Some of them were strangers to our family, but they embraced us by caring enough to exercise their faith, bowing before God to ask for His healing touch on Kyra and me.

Although April and Ben Markham were back in Florida, they carried our crisis with them in their hearts. They sent us a photo from Orlando, where dozens of students had bowed their heads in prayer the previous evening at Discovery Church, rallying with Team Kerr. Our family became known by that name—Team Kerr —and our family of six was a team with more and more players joining us every day. But this was no game, no playful contest—it was a crowd of people putting their hope in God's power.

In North Carolina, my fun-loving, faithful Aunt Peggy kept praying. Years ago, God had impressed upon her the distinct awareness that when she prayed, she would start to see great things. She called my mother on Thursday with some fresh insights that God had granted.

Mom's Journal
Talked to Peggy. Her old pastor had a vision of a strong bright light coming down into her room and going directly into her brain and healing every cell. Praise the Lord for His healing power!

Every member of the McCauley family and all of Team Kerr felt more than ready to receive a surge of strength from God, a burst of light from above that would bring healing. This phone call cast another glimmer of hope on my critical situation, and Aunt Peggy had more to say to my mother, foreshadowing beyond the present crisis of my brain injury.

Mom's Journal
Peggy had the third confirmation of Shannon speaking in front of women, giving her testimony, and people coming up for salvation. We are believing this in the name of Jesus!

It was day eleven, and I was comatose in the ICU, in a life-and-death crisis, and yet there was more at stake than my own life. The crisis in my physical body was part of a larger story, a spiritual one. This horrible injury would pass away, and what would remain would be a true and real testimony to bring spiritual healing to many people. It would become a story of salvation in more ways than one. It was hard for my family to see any of this, standing watch at my bedside, but they believed in the visions that people were sharing with them, and they believed in the God who heals.

The coma persisted, and so did the promises of God. Pastor Justin Mack, too, sensed that my brain injury was a temporary crisis that would result in eternal good. He was the first one to arrive at the ER on the day of the accident and was fully aware of the severity of my condition. As the days wore on, he spoke with Jason in the hospital hallway. "I really believe that Shannon is going to speak to millions," Justin said. "God's got this."

Day after day, Jason's faith didn't waver, and he was confident that God would heal me. But it sure was encouraging to hear reassuring words from others who also saw all the turmoil and trauma through eyes of faith. A telephone call later that day would bring perspective from a person who had seen something else.

Before that phone call, there was another one. Jason stepped away from the ICU and drove to check out the scene of the accident in Castle Rock and to look at the wreckage of the vehicle. While he was driving south toward the fateful intersection, my father called him. "The doctors removed the ventilator," he said. "Shannon is breathing on her own!" My vital signs were steady, and this breakthrough was the good news that Jason needed as he confronted firsthand the wreckage of the van and the sight of the dreadful collision. I was still in a deep coma, but my heart was beating steadily, and Jason's was steadfast as well. He was eager to return to the hospital, more interested in watching me breathe than in focusing on the scrap-metal remains of the accident.

It was a good day. The doctors removed not only the ventilator but also the device that was measuring the pressure on my brain as well as the cooling machine that was regulating my body temperature. Unconscious, my body was at least preserving and maintaining all of the basic functions—and even a little bit beyond the basics. I spontaneously moved my arms and hands, ever so slightly. This was nowhere near the level of activity that my family hoped to see, but it was an amazing, encouraging step forward.

The lyrics of "Oceans" seemed to reverberate around the hospital room, where I lay in bed surrounded by people who cared for me. *Take me deeper than my feet could ever wander, and my faith will be made stronger in the presence of my Savior.* So far my feet were far from being able to take a single step, but I was on a deep, fast-paced adventure of faith in God. While I slept, it was my family and friends, and even total strangers, who had the privilege of trusting God and seeing amazing things unfold. At just the right moments along the way, God was revealing more of His merciful, miraculous ways.

Mike Curry called Jason that day. He is the stranger who had been the second person at the scene of the accident, and his eyewitness account changed the landscape of what had happened. Based on the fragmented information that Jason had heard from Stephanie, he had the foresight to record the phone call, with Mike's permission. Mike owns a woodworking and manufacturing business, but he is trained as a nurse, which means that he had the right kind of coolheaded mind-set to face the entire accident panorama.

Mike's clear-minded observations instantly became a riveting record of a horrible yet extraordinary event. He pulled onto the scene seconds after the crash, and in the horror, there was something mystifyingly magnificent.

He was driving north on Highway 3 on that unforgettable Monday morning, approaching the intersection with 280th Street, where the Castle Rock & Roll Bar & Grill sits on the northeast corner. The surrounding countryside along that road is open fields and grassy terrain. In front of him was another vehicle, and further ahead was a large semitrailer truck. I was driving east on 280th Street.

Mike was a short distance behind the truck and intended to turn left to head west at the intersection. He noticed some commotion up ahead and assumed that someone had dropped something on the road. "I saw this box on the road and a guy pulled over," Mike said. He thought the man was jumping out to get the box, but then the man ran straight toward the bar on the corner.

"And that's when I looked, and then I saw the accident scene," Mike said. His car was not involved in the collision, so he drove to an open lot on the west side of the road and parked. Scrambling quickly out of his car, his heart beating faster than usual, he ran across the street and joined the other man who had hopped out of his own vehicle. The other man had been driving immediately behind the truck, in front of Mike, and he too was unscathed. The only vehicles that crashed were the truck and my van, which had been pushed by the truck up toward a wall on the edge of the property, where the bar's large metal dumpsters sat near the road. The truck had jackknifed and stopped closer to the bar, while the van had kept going about thirty more feet, violently swept up in the momentum of the impact.

As he got closer, Mike heard the van hissing, the engine trying to run but to no avail. The putrid, chemical smells of gasoline, oil, and antifreeze hovered over the ghastly scene. The metal frame of the van was mangled, the windshield shattered, and a smoky, steamy vapor rose in the air. Concerned that the whole fusion of liquid chemical mess might catch on fire, Mike was determined to rescue the passengers before flames engulfed everything. He speedily ran up to the driver-side door.

Then he looked. "There was a person there, kind of slumped

forward, with a light blue top on, sandy-colored hair," Mike told Jason. "The person was just slumped over, not moving, nothing." Jason kept listening.

"And then I looked, and I saw your two girls in the back seat," Mike recounted. "That's when I ran around to the other side, and that's where the glass was actually busted out." Mike and the other man helped to remove Jaydalin from the van. She was actually in the middle of the back seat at that point, although she had been sitting on the left side. They got her out through the back door. Kyra was wedged up against the right-side door, penned in when the impact bent the shell of the van into the space where she sat.

"Your wife, was she wearing a seat belt?" Mike asked.

"Yes," Jason answered.

Mike described the wreckage in more detail. "The whole side of that van was pushed in so hard, it was right up against her,

Minivan totaled

about two feet," he said. "When I was reaching in from the passenger side, your wife was right there in that seat." Jason didn't interrupt.

Repeating himself, Mike went on to tell Jason what he saw. "Your wife was right there in that seat, and there was a person in the driver's seat." Surveying the scenario, Mike spoke to the driver of the other vehicle who had rushed over to help. "The two up front don't look good," Mike remembers saying to the other man, "and the little girl behind the passenger seat doesn't look good."

At that moment, the emergency responders began to arrive, and soon on their heels, the medical helicopter swooped onto the roadway. Mike decided that his involvement was done, so he left and drove tensely to work. Once he arrived at the office, he began telling his coworkers what had happened, exactly like he told the story to Jason. At 1:59 p.m., the local news posted an online article, and other media sources reported on the crash in the ensuing hours. Mike's coworkers read the articles and realized that the newspaper facts weren't matching what he had seen and outlined.

"Mike, there were only three people in that car," his coworkers said to him.

"Oh no," Mike said confidently. "No, no, no, no. There were four. Maybe they have to notify next of kin or something, but there was a fourth person."

And then his coworkers said, "There were two daughters."

"Maybe that was one of the daughters who was in the front seat," Mike replied, trying to make sense of what his coworkers were reporting. But the newspapers had made it clear that the daughters were two little girls, and he had seen two injured adults in the front seat.

Jason heard Mike's account and interjected, "Why do you assume that my wife was in the passenger seat?"

"Because that's where I saw her," Mike answered.

"And there was somebody in the driver's seat?" Jason asked slowly, thinking out loud and grappling with the eyewitness evidence that Mike was disclosing.

"There was somebody in the driver's seat," Mike replied deliberately, with conviction and graciousness in his voice.

Jason kept pondering aloud and asked, "Wearing a light blue—"

"A light blue top, shoulder-length, sandy-colored hair," Mike finished the thought. So the person in the driver's seat was wearing blue? Mike had no idea that I was wearing a red shirt that morning, the same color as the red dress I'd worn at the swing dance on Saturday night, when my long hair had flung around as I stepped freely across the dance floor. "No marks, no bleeding, no movement," Mike went on. "Head slumped over. Never saw her face."

"How old would you guess?" Jason asked. Mike told Jason that he couldn't guess very well because he never saw her face. He thought that the person in the driver's seat was thirty or forty years old. He continued with his assertions.

On day two at work, Mike was talking with his secretary, who was checking the news online. Maybe the journalists would report on all four passengers, now that the sensitive information had been communicated to the family members. "Mike, they only keep talking about three people in that vehicle," his secretary said. Pausing for a moment, she added, "Do you believe in angels?"

"Oh . . ." was all that Mike could say at first. "Those people needed an angel. They still need an angel."

Mike was telling all of this to Jason, and then went back to recounting more of what he had seen. "The weirdest part was, Jason, her leg," Mike started to say, pausing as he described where I was seated in the van, in the passenger seat. "Her left leg was on the driver's side." Mike remembers thinking to himself, *Wow, how did a passenger's leg get over there, on the other side of the shifting console?* It was very peculiar to him in that instant. Mike told Jason that he had a hard time getting the accident scene out of his mind.

"Wow, was that an angel?" Mike asked, speaking his thoughts aloud as he talked with Jason. "I really don't know, but there was a fourth person," Mike asserted. As he continued to reflect on the facts, Mike was convinced that it was an angel. He wondered if I have a sister, a cousin, a friend, somebody who died, somebody who was there to protect me. Mike voiced the questions in his mind, and those questions hung in the air, unanswered, as the two of them talked on the phone.

"Jaydalin doesn't really remember how she got out of the vehicle," Jason said to Mike. Jason had heard from the other emergency responders that Jaydalin was screaming and yelling and that Kyra might have been moaning.

At first, Kyra wasn't doing anything, Mike observed. Then she started moaning, just kind of a whimper. Initially the van was only steaming, with smoke puffing out of the engine, then all of a sudden after about three minutes, the horn started blowing. Mike was describing the blaring noise, while Jason was still curious about the unidentified passenger.

"Did you guys break the window behind the passenger door or behind the driver's door to get in?" Jason asked.

"That's what they were going to do," Mike replied. He was attending to Kyra and me on the passenger side. The other responders wanted to pull Kyra out right away, but Mike warned them that she was stuck. Freeing her from the wreckage would require the extraction tools that they promptly employed as he was leaving.

Jason was piecing together the puzzle. He knew that the DVD player in the van was mounted up front, above the middle console. Most likely, my head hit the DVD player when I was brutally thrust from one side of the van to the other. Mike didn't recall anything about that specifically, but he continued to reflect on what he had seen.

"You know, one thing was weird—I didn't see any airbags in the front," Mike said. "Had they gone off?"

"When I was there today," Jason answered, "the steering wheel one was open, with blood on it." Jason told Mike what the police officer had later reported to him. Apparently one of the airbags had not activated, but on the right side they had deployed.

"Yes," Mike agreed. "Those airbags were hanging down in the window, because I had to keep moving them to even see inside."

They were less concerned about the mechanics of the airbags and more interested to talk more about the people inside. Jason wanted to know if Jaydalin said anything to Mike, but she was in too much shock, looking around at all of the strangers huddled around the scene. When Jason had arrived at the hospital, Jaydalin knew who her father was, but she wasn't totally coherent.

"She wasn't saying anything," Mike related. "She wasn't crying." It was a relief for Jason to know that his little girl was all right in the care of these good Samaritans.

"So when you left," Jason went on, "there was still that extra person in the front seat."

Mike's response was affirmative. "Yeah, the whole time I was there, there were four people in that vehicle."

"You left before they tried to get my wife or anybody out of the car?" Jason asked.

"Right," Mike answered. He reiterated that when the professional responders arrived, they started to take over the accident scene.

Jason couldn't resist wondering about the fourth person. "Why wouldn't somebody have tried to get the person who was in the driver's seat?" he asked.

Mike calmly described the atmosphere, where most of the people were mere onlookers. Nobody was really helping at first. He and the other man were the only ones close to the van until the professional emergency responders arrived. Without training and equipment, there wasn't much else that he and the other man could do.

"You got Jaydalin out," Jason said, digging for more information. He was still thinking about the other passengers and asked Mike about his strategy. Why didn't they try immediately to remove the person who was slumped over at the steering wheel?

"I was on the passenger side," Mike said. He reflected back on his recollection of everything that happened in that split-second moment. "I don't know." Mike remembered that as the emergency crews arrived, there were people trying to break a window. He was focused on trying to attend to me.

"Shannon was never coherent, right?" Jason said soberly.

"Oh no," Mike said. "I didn't think she would make it." His tone was sympathetic and wistful as he spoke. "She was breathing about three times a minute and gasping every time she breathed.

It wasn't a fluid breath; it was more of a very labored breath. And then nothing for . . ."

Mike's background as a nurse equipped him to assess my condition, or at least the essentials, from his position outside. He knew that it was not good. And the way the vehicle was crushed, it was impossible to really access the inside of the seating area to perform CPR or anything like that. "How sad, how sad," he said to Jason. "You've been in my prayers. There's a lot of people in your corner."

"Do you have any more on the lady who was in the driver's seat?" Jason asked.

"No," Mike responded. "I couldn't reach over there because I was on the passenger side."

"Did you look to see if this lady was breathing or making noise or anything?"

Mike answered with certainty. "There was no movement, no nothing," he said. "I actually thought she was dead." From his vantage point, he was looking for signs that her chest was rising but saw no indication that she was alive. Mike said that the entire event was undoubtedly a unique experience for him. He was still putting his own pieces together.

Jason understood that feeling, as he too was not sure what to think of everything. Reaching out across the phone, Jason asked, "Can I pray with you?"

"You bet," Mike answered.

The raw faith of my husband rose clearly through the phone and to the ears of God as he proceeded to pray, his words expressing gratitude and confidence. Jason was convinced that the God who saves us from death and gives us eternal life was with us in this heartbreaking life-and-death experience.

"Lord, thank You for Mike, just his willingness to be obedient in that moment and try to help my family. Thank You for all You're doing in healing Kyra. Thank You for protecting Jayda. Continue to heal and restore my wife, Lord, and whatever this fourth person could have been, just thank You for Your covering,

Lord. Thank You for Your protection. Thank You for who You are and what You continue to do, Lord. Thank You for dying for us and just giving us that free gift of salvation. You are mighty. We give You all the praise. We don't know why these things happen, but thank You for Mike's willingness to help in that moment. In Your name, amen.

"Amen," Mike added. "So, you said your wife has a trach now. Is she still in a coma?"

"Yes, sir," Jason said.

"She is," Mike said quietly, letting the news sink in. "OK."

Jason rebounded, expressing his faith again. "We're praying for a full recovery for her, that the Lord will just touch her in an instant and—"

"And we know He can," Mike affirmed.

"That's right, that's right, I have no doubt," Jason said. "So I ask for you to pray if it comes to your mind, if you think anything of it, to pray for my wife, Shannon, and thank Him for the healing of Kyra and continual healing for her."

"I've been praying for you guys all day long," Mike said. "It doesn't leave my mind, it really doesn't."

As he hung up the phone, it didn't leave Jason's mind, either. Who was this fourth person? There was no doubt that Mike had seen something extraordinary, something that he could never have invented. Mike knew nothing about our family that day as he drove to work and had no need to imagine an outlandish story. He described every detail with solid serenity, and since then his testimony hasn't changed. It was documentation for a miracle, mystifying and wonderful.

The intersection of two ordinary roads in Castle Rock, Minnesota, became the extraordinary, supernatural intersection of heaven and earth. It is beyond explanation. An easygoing Monday morning trip to see a puppy turned into an intriguing, glorious sight that no one could have envisioned. In between, before the moment of wonder, was a horrific crash. Mike ran to the accident scene, determined to help us, and we were mere strangers to him. Edging closer, he looked at someone who was a stranger to all of us, a fourth person who doesn't really exist on this earth. We can only think that he saw an angel.

Why did God place that fourth person with us? Just days before, Jason had prompted people to read and pray through Psalm 91. "For he will command his angels concerning you to guard you in all your ways" (Psalm 91:11). At first glance, traumatic brain injury does not seem like a dramatic, supernatural rescue by a guardian angel. There has to be more to this story than that! To understand what really happened, we can only turn our eyes to God and trust that He was doing something amazing to care for us, beyond what anyone could see firsthand.

The angelic presence was a glimpse of God's love. "'What no eye has seen, what no ear has heard, and what no human mind has conceived'—the things God has prepared for those who love him—these are the things God has revealed to us by his Spirit" (1 Corinthians 2:9-10). As Jason says, we must love God through the hard times. And as those hard times continued, God revealed to me and to my family some eye-opening insights. Looking closely at what happened, and looking to God, we began to see more clearly His loving purposes.

That would come later, and this was Thursday. Like Jason had told Mike, I was still sleeping, but it had been a good day. There was the fascinating reality of angels in our midst, which alone was enough to buoy my family forward. And I was breathing on my own, a milestone demonstrating that I was not sinking but maybe even beginning to rise above the waves. *You call me out upon the waters . . . and there I find You in the mystery.* "Oceans" was the perfect backdrop within the walls of my hospital room, singing of mysteries and claiming that my plunge into a coma was a story of God's care. *Your grace abounds in deepest waters, Your sovereign hand will be my guide.*

Kyra, too, was gaining ground. She moved from the ICU to the pediatric unit, assigned to a large room with a couch and two beds. This extra space meant that Jaydalin would be able to spend the night—a fun sleepover for two sisters instead of a scary hospitalization. The room was next to the children's playroom, and Kyra sat at the piano, her gray-haired grandpa Terry by her side, her colorful polka-dotted blanket draped over her lap.

A large team of medical staff—nurses, dietician, interns, physical therapist, and occupational therapist—met with Jason and the family to review Kyra's prognosis. They reported that her internal organs were healing, and they expected to remove her feeding tube once her appetite increased. She was still being medicated for the pain of her injuries, but the diminishing dosage was a sign that she was on the mend. Another robust indication of Kyra's healing was all of the games that she played with visitors. For Jason, playing Zingo with his little girl was a delight beyond description. The playroom in the pediatric wing of the hospital became a lively oasis, where a relieved father dispensed game tiles and fun as his daughter's young mind quickly raced to be the first player with a full card and then yell, "Zingo!"

My mother summarized the day's developments in a sentence, saying all that really needed to be said.

Mom's Journal
We are praising God for all His goodness today!

The fun of the playroom was a stark contrast to the roller-coaster ride of my recovery. My brother Dan took a turn at updating the CaringBridge® website on Friday, substituting for Kristi. "Shannon is taking a break from breathing on her own," Dan reported bluntly. "She is getting assistance." He didn't go into details about my fragility. Instead, he followed up with an urgent appeal for people to keep praying for my brain to heal. "Please keep praying that God will restore Shannon and bring her back to us."

Life is like that—it's a roller-coaster ride. The ups and downs are the norm on this earth, where elation and discouragement are part of the everyday journey. One day my family was thrilled to see me breathing on my own and amazed by the eyewitness account of the angel. The next day they watched as I struggled to stay alive, unable to inhale oxygen by myself. But Dan also said in that same CaringBridge® post, "Faith isn't believing that God can do something—it's knowing He will!"

On the plus side, Kyra was rebounding, literally. She dunked basketballs and kicked soccer balls in physical therapy, excited to be up on her feet after so many days in bed. The nurses added to Kyra's fun, giving her a toy syringe that she used as a water gun, squirting my mother and my brother Mike. I wish I could have heard her giggling!

Between playfully dodging water from Kyra's attacks with the toy water gun and soberly sitting by my bedside, my mother kept turning her thoughts to God. She sensed the contrast between the positive progress and the stagnant void of my coma. It was overwhelming, and she penned a prayer in her journal.

Mom's Journal

Lord, I am asking You to heal our daughter totally and completely. I pray that the visions of people that have been confirmed by more than one would be fulfilled. My flesh feels weak today, so I am claiming where I am weak You are strong! Help me, Lord, to be strong in You.

SATURDAY
September 26, 2015

The days flowed together, one after another. My mother's journal went on, page after page.

> **Mom's Journal**
> Shannon, you are sitting up this morning. Dad said your eyes are open a little more, but you aren't focusing yet. But we know you are trying.

I was beginning to move my eyelids! But it was too soon to see anything, and far too soon to jump for joy. As if things weren't bad enough, I was diagnosed with a bladder infection and pneumonia. Pneumonia is a scary condition for a person who is barely breathing in the first place. My mother was freaked out by the idea. But my father received some input from the medical staff and reassured her that nearly 100 percent of people with brain trauma get pneumonia. "I hate every minute of this," my mother responded. Then she promptly added, "The positive has been God's presence."

My mother longed to watch over me but spent most of the day and night with Kyra, who had occupational therapy at 9:00 a.m., followed by plenty of playtime with her sister, Jaydalin. When it was nap time in the afternoon, my mother was ready to rest too. My mother later scribbled in her journal about the day's activities.

> **Mom's Journal**
> Grandma took a little nap. I am so tired. Lord, I need Your continued strength.

My father camped out in my room, keeping vigil. He wanted to be the one by my side when I eventually woke up. My mother had something to say about this, too, in her journal.

Mom's Journal
Dad says you're going to talk to him first. I hope that
happens for him. He doesn't like leaving his Baby Girl for
very long! We are all missing you desperately!! I pray with
everything in me you open your eyes soon. Love you so
much!!

Her anguished punctuation wasn't enough to rouse me, but
my mother's love and the love of God sustained me in the silent
interlude. Tomorrow would be another day.

Today was another day. Things were looking bleak again. And, just as He had done before when the gloomy darkness threatened to settle into the scene, God sent another angel.

My mother noted that she started the day in Kyra's room, munching on some fruit and sensing that God was there, in the hospital, working powerfully, even though unseen. That was reason enough to rejoice, and she reflected on God's presence as she added more lines to her journal.

For Kyra, it was a lively day, with school friends visiting throughout the afternoon. Her beaming smile assured everyone that she would soon be back to join them in the school classroom and on the playground during recess time. Even though she was engrossed in the excitement, Kyra was well aware that I was missing in the line of visitors. She sent a message to me: "Make sure Grandpa tells Mommy that I love her!"

What Kyra didn't know was that my condition was pretty hopeless that day. My father remembers the feeling of despair that edged into his heart as evening fell. I wasn't moving—I wasn't doing anything. It seemed to him that I was actually getting worse.

The hushed hum of the medical equipment was my father's companionship as he sat by my bedside. Evening turned to night, and it was 10:00 p.m. A nurse was conducting her patient rounds and entered my room to change my medical briefs. My father always preferred to step outside while the nurses handled these types of duties, so he walked down the hallway, praying for his helpless daughter as he paced the halls.

He would pray for other hospital patients, too, during these long hours of vigil. Exercising his faith, my father put his hope in God's healing power, not just for me but also for them. He wandered toward the empty room of a woman who had been discharged from the hospital and paused at the doorway, glancing inside.

My father stopped to look more closely when he saw a custodian cleaning the room. The custodian was a white-haired black man, perhaps seventy years old, hunched over but agile as he mopped the floor like a young sailor scrubbing the deck of a ship. The late hour was nothing to this man as he briskly made the tile floor shine under the glaring fluorescent lights.

As my father looked, mindlessly observing the diligent worker, the custodian glanced up and made eye contact with him. The man looked intently at my father and paused, the soapy water puddling on the floor near his feet. "She's going to be OK," the custodian said. Seeing my father's blank stare, he went on. "It's going to be OK, just leave it up to Him."

And that was all that the custodian said. Dumbfounded, my father only uttered a feeble "Yeah," then walked past the doorway and back into my room.

The nurse had finished tending to my needs, and my father leaned against the radiator in my room, reflecting on what had just happened. *That man knew exactly what I was thinking*, my father pondered. The custodian's words struck him so much that my father straightened up and walked back down the hall to talk with the man again.

But the custodian was gone. My father searched in other nearby rooms but couldn't find him. He urgently wanted to talk again with this man who had instilled in his heart a glimmer of hope on a dark and cheerless night. As my father returned to the quiet of my room, he realized that all along throughout my hospital stay he had noticed several Somalian immigrant women, each of them probably thirty to thirty-five years old, who cleaned the rooms. They would mop the floors regularly, and over a period of days, my father had begun to recognize them and converse with them. He had never seen this older custodian before, and never saw him again.

No one else was cleaning the rooms that late at night, only a soft-spoken, kind-hearted, intriguingly mysterious man. As quickly as the floor had dried, the custodian had completely disappeared.

Was this another angel? He had delivered a message that directed my father's focus toward the hope of God's healing touch. *She's going to be OK . . . she will be healed.* Two mystifying messengers had appeared in the hospital—the man from Swaziland in colorful attire and now this dark-skinned, white-haired custodian whose eyes shone brighter than the floor he was cleaning—both with the same message at a moment when my crisis seemed most dismal. Both had vanished, but their words of encouragement remained, assuring my family that their faith in God's healing was not in vain. In the midst of gloomy darkness, there was hope. God was clearly making Himself known in extraordinary ways that cannot be explained from a human perspective. And not only were there exceptional encounters in the hospital but also an angel alongside me in the van during the accident. Undoubtedly, God was in the process of telling a very real and transcendent story through a very real and earthly experience. It would be worth the long wait of the vigil to see how the story would end.

Dreary as the day had been, with my father's assessment that I was actually getting worse, the fact is that at least I was opening my eyes that day. When my father looked at me, he sadly couldn't see the Shannon that he knows, but he clung to the hope that God really would heal me. My mother shared the same hope that night, making note of the delicate tension between looking face-first at the miserable ordeal and seeing traces of a desired, joyful outcome.

Mom's Journal

Shannon, you have been opening your eyes a lot today, but you aren't there. Dad says it's so hard for him to see your beautiful brown eyes but not see you! We know you are there somewhere, and we are going to rejoice big-time when you come back to us!

At 3:16 a.m., my brother Dan—I call him Danny—posted an update on YouTube, publishing it with these key words to trigger any searches online: Shannon Kerr, Faith, God, Love. He added a hashtag, too: #McCauleyKerrStrong. Dan spoke for thirteen minutes, facing the camera and putting a strong message of faith in front of anyone who would discover the video on the Internet.

YouTube Message

Prayer works, and God is real. Prayer is all Jason wants and all he's been doing, crying out to God to save his girls.

Shannon is my sister. Shannon and Jason have a powerful marriage. Within the last forty-eight hours, Shannon has started to open her eyes just a little bit. We believe that Shannon is coming back. She needs prayer.

The doctors tell us that technically she isn't there. Our God is going to completely restore her, and we know this. Shannon is going to come back swinging because that's what Shannon does. She's the strongest person I know. Shannon would be slapping us around, saying, "Why are you worried? I'm with the Lord."

God doesn't take away our problems, but He makes it easier to get through. The greatest gift we have is our Savior. Regardless of if you truly believe in God or not, He loves you anyway. If you're struggling with anything, I'm telling you right now, God is real, God hears your cry, and God answers prayer.

God loves you so much. Through all your trials and all the stuff you're going through, He died for you to take away your pain. He was on the cross with all the stripes on His back because He was whipped. The Bible clearly states that by His stripes we are healed.

Shannon is going to be healed, and I pray that if you need healing, you will find true healing in God.

The message that Dan voiced for all to hear via YouTube echoed so many of the thoughts that my family holds close in our hearts, and it echoed the words of the angelic messengers whom God had sent to encourage everyone. Being McCauley Kerr Strong means having a strength that is not our own! We are strong because of God, and just as Dan said, God is real. For now, what everyone needed to do was keep praying, waiting for God to perform His powerful work of healing.

At 3:00 a.m., at the same time that Dan was recording and posting his video, my mother woke up in Kyra's hospital room to an incessant beeping noise. The alarm was emitted by Kyra's feeding tube, and it was not medically alarming, only a nuisance that awakened my mother to another day of waiting and praying. My mother lay awake until 6:00 a.m. in the spare bed near her sleeping granddaughter, unable to sleep but tirelessly persisting in prayer. Little did she know that her son had just posted another urgent appeal for people to pray.

Coming back swinging—as Dan had said I would do—was not on my horizon anytime soon, although I was moving my eyes and arms just a little bit. I was still comatose, and the hospital staff seemed to be acting as if that was as good as it would ever get. According to the doctors' reports, the best-case scenario was that I would open my eyes. It was as if I were beyond any hope of further recovery.

That afternoon at 1:00 p.m., the doctors met with my family and recommended that I be transferred to another medical facility. Since my vital signs remained steady, the next step was to undergo rehabilitation for my brain, or at least to try. It seemed like a futile attempt, but it was the only real option. Jason agreed to authorize the move. The hospital staff put the paperwork into motion to proceed with arrangements for my transfer. Meanwhile, the McCauley Kerr Strong crowd kept firm in their hope that the prospect of my brain awakening was not out of the question. The question was when?

Already, Kyra's vast improvement was an indication of God's healing touch. The beeping signal that had started the day was soon obsolete because Kyra no longer needed medical equipment to sustain her. Within a few hours, the doctors removed Kyra's feeding tube, and by the end of the day she was eating one of her favorite foods—pizza. Jason's mother, Kristine, spent the night at the hospital with Kyra, while my parents went home. Just like Jason, my father's management responsibilities at Jimmy John's had been accumulating for the past two weeks, so he hesitantly stepped away from the hospital overnight to catch up on some of the workload. At least this time he had the positive expectation that Kyra would soon be skipping into one of his Jimmy John's shops to eat a sandwich again.

My parents took Jaydalin home with them overnight and stopped by our house in Lakeville to pick up her cherished blanket. My mother jotted a sidebar in her journal about that brief stop at the house, writing as if I would later read those pages.

Mom's Journal

We took Jayda home with us. We had to stop at the Kerrs' to get her blanket. When we were leaving, I walked over to the red rocking chairs where you always do your devotions, Shan. You have a bowl of painted rocks in there, and the thing that caught my eye was the rock that said: Never Give Up! That's where we are standing!

The nurses had me sitting up in my hospital bed for two hours again on Monday, to ease the flow of oxygen in my lungs. It had been too long since I had sat in my red rocking chair on the front porch in Lakeville, reading my Bible and filling my soul with strength from God's Word. But, breath after breath, there was no giving up, even in a hospital in downtown Minneapolis.

At 3:00 p.m. on Tuesday, we reached a milestone—all three of us Kerr girls had vacated Hennepin County Medical Center. After sixteen days in the hospital, Kyra was discharged, her big, beaming smile broadcasting not only her happiness but also her healing. Jason drove Kyra home, and the joy on her face as she sat next to Jaydalin in the back seat was a bold contrast to the jolting catastrophe that they had experienced. Kyra hugged her colorful polka-dotted blanket on the ride home, its soft fleece a cheerful comfort, reminding her that she was wrapped in love and care.

Kyra in wheelchair with Jason in hallway

Our two little girls had been through a lot of hardship since the last time they had sat side by side, blankets closely cuddled, on another roadway, on another trip. Now that journey was behind them, and they were a living testimony to God's healing. They would never forget the extraordinary events surrounding their ordinary trip to see a puppy on September 14 — and they would never forget that God had protected their lives. Kyra said to our friend Ben Markham what she would say to many others, "Thank you so much for praying for me." My mother, too, could not contain her gratitude when she wrote in her journal.

Mom's Journal
Another miracle! Kyra is going home today! Lord, You are so amazing. Your goodness and grace keep us going!

We can't explain how they survived the impact of the collision —we can only be grateful. As my own journey of healing continued, we would learn more about God's protective care on that fateful Monday morning. In the meantime, at least we knew we were alive, and that was reason to rejoice. Kyra was very excited to go home, and my family had a small celebration at Buffalo Wild Wings that evening.

At the same time that Kyra was released, I too was released to another medical facility and traveled by ambulance to Bethesda Hospital in St. Paul, the twin city of Minneapolis. Bethesda is a long-term acute care hospital that is known for its work with brain trauma patients. The strategy was to implement a regimen of physical and occupational therapy to boost my possibility of recovery.

I was oblivious to all of this, but Jason told my mother that I did track his movement slightly with my eyes as he stood over my bed talking to me about our children. I didn't hear his words, nor was I aware of anything. Lying flat on plain, white hospital sheets, my hair shaved short and my neck in a tight brace, I was no poster child of healing. But there was life in me, and being at a medical facility that could challenge my capacities was the perfect place for a person like me. That's who I am. I like to put it like this: *You always push. You don't wuss out. You push forward and keep going.* I wasn't going to settle for sitting back on the couch. I play to win!

The scene at our house in Lakeville was as active as mine was dormant, with the girls at home and the boys in school. Kyra stayed home from school, playing with LEGOs, while Jaydalin played a memory game with her grandpa Terry. Jason and my father put their heads together to handle the family finances, which is something that I usually do. Jason was on the run a lot during those days, doing an amazing job at being a father to our four children, while all four grandparents helped as much as they could. My mother kept a written record of many of the comings and goings while I was immobilized.

Mom's Journal
It takes a lot of people to cover what you do every day, Shannon. We need you back.

I certainly wasn't back yet, but my medical condition was showing signs of improvement. I was breathing on my own without the ventilator, and amazingly, I began to move my left leg a bit. It was a fitting development for the day when I was about to begin a systematic therapy plan.

Brenda Boatman, my occupational therapist, had been at Bethesda for more than twenty years, focusing her work on people with brain and neural injuries. Before she met me, Brenda examined my medical chart and immediately had a positive impression based on the profile information that was at her fingertips. Brenda recognized from the start that I'm a very fit and active person—not your typical thirty-seven-year-old—and she went in with an open mind, ready to do whatever she could to coach me back toward health. She was determined, even though my case would be difficult.

"Shannon was very impaired," Brenda later admitted. I still

had a helmet on my head, a patch over my right eye, and a stiff brace supporting my neck. My right arm wasn't moving at all. But Brenda said that there was immediately something exceptional about her initial interaction with me. "I noticed a bright spot in her left eye," Brenda said. "There was something there." Somehow, with her two decades of experience, she was able to distinguish a glimpse of my zest for life. That first observation was an impulse for Brenda, striking her as unusual.

Brenda soon began to take special interest in my crisis. She also met Jason and my father on that first day of therapy, becoming aware of my solid family context as well as my strong spiritual background. Brenda knew that these factors were vital to my rehabilitation. "Jason was so involved and loving," Brenda told us afterward. "He wanted knowledge and asked a lot of questions, so I educated him on positive indicators." Brenda partnered with us —she joined Team Kerr in her own professional and skillful ways.

Since Brenda is a runner, too, she understood my competitive mind-set as well as the crushing defeat of being bedridden and comatose. Learning about my physical and mental abilities from my family and from her firsthand observation, Brenda knew how to motivate me. She heard that I was in the habit of intensive running and that I liked to do P90X athletic workout routines on my own. I was used to pushing past my limits. Brenda was committed to making that possible again. She began with basic, familiar movements, retraining my limbs to perform actions that had once been so easy. As the days wore on, even while I was still in a somnolent coma, Brenda kept reminding me that I am fighter.

Brenda was right. Yes, it's true that I am known as a fighter— and also as a friend. I tell about this only because of how all of it came into play when I was comatose, unable to run and unable to reach out to the people I love.

I don't talk about my athletic victories unless people ask me, but my competitive spirit was a crucial component in my recovery process. When I was in seventh grade, I ran the

100-meter race in an event where the varsity coach happened to be there timing the runners. When he saw my speed, the coach was shocked and spoke with my father, asking if he would allow me to run with the high school team. My father granted me permission to go for it. The school then began to bring a bus to the middle school to pick me up and shuttle me to the high school track practice. I ran the 100-meter, the 200-meter, and the relay races for both of those distances, from seventh through twelfth grades. In twelfth grade, the team voted for me to be the captain, and that same school year I was also captain of the basketball team. In basketball, I played the wing position. I liked playing defense and stealing the ball—and going in for a layup to score. Dribbling through the pressure, speeding down the track, I pushed through the chaotic field to the end.

I became known as the fastest girl in my hometown of Owatonna, and the community was with me. Some of the senior citizens in town would come to the high school games to watch me play. My thrill wasn't only about the trophies or the applause, because I loved the team and the many people I met along the way. Having my picture in the newspaper was fun, but making other people smile was even better.

My love for people outlived my high school sports medals and extended past graduation. I like to include people in my joys and successes, to talk and laugh and, yes, to pray with them. Bringing people together comes naturally to me, and I would be the best friend of everybody if that were possible. When the coma stripped away all of those abilities, the relationships held steady, and people reached out to me instead. Instead of sharing in a success, they were sharing in my suffering, giving me a warm smile or gentle hug at the hospital.

As an occupational therapist, Brenda quickly perceived all of this, understanding what kind of person I am. She was an excellent therapist, and she expended endless energy, trying to help me get back on my feet. Somehow along the way, she joined in the crowd of people who were supporting me wholeheartedly, not just professionally. She also knew how to have a good time, adding doses of humor to the therapy sessions. Fully versed in the practices of her field, Brenda grasped the magnitude of what was happening, beyond my physical statistics. "There is no medical reason that Shannon survived," Brenda said many months later, acknowledging that my healing process exceeded expectations. She obviously loves her job and also the opportunity that it gives her to watch the extraordinary unfold. "I get to see miracles happen," Brenda said.

There was no guarantee that I would be one of the success stories—quite the opposite. Miracles happen, but not as the norm. The doctors told my family that at any point along the way, my progress could come to a complete halt. I might never walk, let alone run. It was all very much a walk of faith, for my family and for me. For now, walking wasn't even anyone's concern yet, because I was still asleep and barely opening my eyes. On that first full day at Bethesda, though, the outlook was starting to brighten. Jason picked up the framed photo from the Saturday night swing dance, and I vaguely followed that image with my eyes. *Where feet may fail and fear surrounds me, You've never failed and You won't start now.* My feet were failing, but God had not failed me. There was no need to fear. And there was hope in Jason's heart that my feet would even dance with his again.

In order to ever have vitality to swing dance, I would need wholesome nourishment in keeping with my athletic lifestyle. Jason and I have educated ourselves in healthy nutrition and have passed those practices on to our children. I love chocolate and am happy to munch on a warm homemade cookie, just like the ones that Kyra and I baked on the Sunday night before the accident. But I generally cook organic foods for my family and avoid buying products that contain more than five ingredients. Food is fuel, so it must be packed with nutrients, not junk! Because of this, Jason was appalled at the nutritional supplement that the hospital administered to me.

At Hennepin County Medical Center, they hooked me up to

a bag of liquid food that was made from high-fructose corn syrup and other artificial ingredients. It was manufactured by a well-known brand that also makes chocolate chips, but it was neither luscious chocolate nor was it a solid source of nutrition. It had a long shelf life, which made it convenient. What I needed was some power food, not a syrupy, artificial concoction that would barely sustain my vegetative state. Jason questioned the value of their methods, especially when it began to affect my blood sugar levels. I have never been diabetic, but suddenly the nurses were testing my blood every four hours and administering insulin to regulate my blood sugar.

Jason wondered how the hospital's dieticians expected me to heal if the sugary supplement was my only source of nourishment. So he did his own research. Determined to provide me with good nutrition, Jason found an organic whole foods product called Liquid Hope that would be a better meal replacement alternative. However, since it was not packaged in a sealed bag, it had to be poured through a funnel into one of the hospital's bags. This process posed a high risk of cross-contamination with bacteria, and the nurses warned Jason that he might be jeopardizing my safety. So he opted against the risk.

But when I transferred to Bethesda, Jason talked with the hospital staff at this new location, expressing again his concern about providing me with wholesome nutrition. He calmly but firmly objected to the idea of feeding me the sugary supplement, or poison, as I would call it. The nurses agreed to make the change, implementing the new regimen of Liquid Hope. Right away, my blood levels stabilized, and there was no more need for the insulin treatments. The organic supplement was expensive, but Jason was convinced that it was a worthwhile investment. Liquid Hope was not only a gesture to feed me well, it constituted Jason's confident hope that one day I would use that energy to wake up from the coma and have a solid grip on life again.

So, with the initiation of a therapy program and the introduction of a wholesome nutritional supplement, some of my medical circumstances seemed to be on the upswing at Bethesda. But, to put it all into perspective, the coma still hung over everything. And the incessant vigil was weighing on my family, too. My mother wrote in her journal about the agony of watching the entire struggle, even in the midst of trusting that God would heal me. Every breath was part of the struggle.

Mom's Journal

They put you in a chair today. When we went back down to the room, Dad was not happy! Your neck was not being supported, and you needed to be suctioned out. Your breathing and heart rate were up. They had to nebulize you and then gave you something to relax you. This all kind of tipped your mother over the top of life. I hate watching you go through all of this. I wish it didn't have to be. Even with all of this, they say you are physically stable! Lord, we need Your miracle power! By Your stripes she is healed!

Each individual in the family had to find ways to cope with the implications of the coma. They were helpless to fix the problem on their own, but they knew that their ultimate help was in God —and that underlying hope carried them onward, day after day. Jason got into the habit of listening to the song "Anchor" by Hillsong Worship as he drove back and forth to the hospital. While my favorite song talks of rising above the waves of the oceans, the lyrics that struck his heart were a grounding anchor through the raging waters of our calamity.

I have this hope
As an anchor for my soul
Through every storm
I will hold to You

With endless love
All my fear is swept away

In everything
I will trust in You

There is hope in the promise of the cross
You gave everything to save the world You love
And this hope is an anchor for my soul
Our God will stand
Unshakable

Unchanging One
You who was and is to come
Your promise sure
You will not let go

Your Name is higher
Your Name is greater
All my hope is in You
Your word unfailing
Your promise unshaken
All my hope is in You

In deepest oceans and crashing storms, both Jason and I knew that God was our firm hope. On the morning of September 14, at the intersection in Castle Rock, life as we knew it had changed drastically, but God would not let go of us! There was something about the angel on the scene that would mean more to us in days to come. Soon enough, I would personally learn more about God's purposes in saving my life in such a dramatic way. For now, we needed to rest. For Jason, resting meant trusting God's promises of healing, and for me, resting meant remaining in the ongoing sleep of the coma.

At Bethesda, none of my family members were allowed to spend the night. They made up for it by filling up the daytimes to the maximum, never leaving me alone. Jason would come throughout the morning, and then my father would sit with me in the evenings.

For Jason, sitting by my bedside in silence was a grim contrast to our normal morning conversations. Jason often plays pickup basketball in the morning, and when he returns home, I usually ask about his game. "What did you do on the court?" I always want to know. "Did you stuff anybody?" Even a noncompetitive pickup basketball game is worth turning into a friendly but fierce competition! We are a family that plays hard. Now it was up to Jason to push forward on his own, without hearing the cheerful banter of his biggest fan.

Jason and I met because of basketball. It was March of my junior year of high school, and Jason was a college freshman who studied at Pillsbury Baptist Bible College and played basketball in my hometown of Owatonna. On the day we met, I was going with two of my girlfriends to watch the Owatonna varsity team play in Rochester. I had specifically told my friends that I didn't want them to invite any boys to join us, but they did—and Jason was one of the two boys. There was no way to uninvite the boys at that point, so I tried to be friendly and make the most of it. I went straight to the point, posing a thought-provoking question and not wasting time with small talk.

"So, what do you guys believe in?" I asked.

Jason was in the back of the group, tall as ever. He was the only one who spoke up, saying, "Well, we believe in Jesus."

"That's awesome!" I exclaimed. Hearing that Jason believed in Jesus was all that it took to change my opinion about the boys being there that day, and it changed my thoughts about him in particular. I love Jesus, and there was something very likable about this boy! There was one small problem, though, because my father prohibited me from dating college guys when I was still in high school.

Thankfully, that problem was soon overcome because my parents liked Jason, too. They liked how respectful he was, addressing them as Mr. and Mrs. McCauley, and Jason really liked my three younger brothers. So when Jason asked me on a first date, my father said I could go, even though he had just denied the request of another college boy the previous month. Jason planned to return to his home in Michigan in May after the spring semester and not come back to Pillsbury, but meeting me changed all of that. He stayed in the area, working while I finished twelfth grade. When I graduated from high school in 1997, both Jason and I went to St. Cloud Technical and Community College in Minnesota and got two-year degrees. We kept playing basketball throughout college, and we kept dating. Our wedding was in 1999, and our life together, which had begun centered on Jesus, was off to a wonderful start.

And now, here we were in 2015, and this was no twenty-second time-out in a lively basketball game. It was a standstill, and Jason was celebrating small victories, sitting by my bedside. He later told my mother about the day's wins, and she was content to be reporting on another episode in the life of her beloved son-in-law and daughter.

Mom's Journal

Jason came up this morning as he always does. He felt encouraged by what he saw. He was wiping your eyes, and you were closing them for him. The staff said it seems like you are trying to wake up! We are believing that you are doing just that.

The victories seemed so small. Opening and closing my eyes was a feat so much different than a game-winning three-point shot, but it was all according to God's master game plan. Just as

God had indicated earlier, the breakthrough from my coma was not going to be swift.

On day one, Aunt Peggy had sensed Jesus saying that my healing would not be instantaneous. Now that we were in October, Liz Matson, Peggy's daughter-in-law, had another vision. God instilled in her an undeniable understanding that I would not only be healed but also have a message to share with many people. Liz recounted the divine vision, saying, "God put in my heart that Shannon will be a voice to the nations, but how long it will take will be part of the story." Vision after vision, day after day, God confirmed to my family that even when things look bleak, He is working on it in unseen ways. Amazingly, He allowed us to look and see more than we ever imagined.

My family waited to see what God would do next. I was sitting in a chair when my parents arrived at Bethesda at 2:30 p.m. They brought me down to the sitting room, where they talked and sang to me. My mother read Scriptures about healing out loud, while my father tenderly held my left hand. Actually, he was pleased that there was also a practical need to hold my hand. I was moving it! Compulsively, I kept trying to lift my hand to touch my tracheostomy tube, and my father was holding me back from causing any damage to the tube. After so many days of immobility, I seemed to be having no trouble moving my left side, although my right side was not moving much at all. Even in the void of the vigil, my mother's journal took a lighthearted spin that evening.

Mom's Journal
It's around 5:30 p.m. Jason came back up. He brought Dad and me each a fast-food hamburger for dinner. You wouldn't approve of that, Shannon. Wake up and protest what we are eating!

Now I hear from my mother about the junk food that they were eating while I was totally unaware! On a family vacation in my childhood, we had eaten cheeseburgers every day for two weeks.

I had eaten more than enough cheeseburgers and avoided them ever since. I would never touch a burger like that now. I would jokingly call it poison! And this is what makes Jason's care that much more special. He was an advocate for my nutritional needs, fully embracing what is important to me, and doing everything he could to ensure that the girl he met on the basketball court would one day be able to play again.

In the outside world, beyond the walls of Bethesda, it was a big day. The school that Trenton, Braylon, and Kyra were attending held its annual Jog-a-Thon fund-raiser to support the elementary-level programs. Each year, the students sign up to run laps in the school gymnasium, and their grandparents pay a donation per lap that they complete.

Kyra hadn't gone back to school yet, but she made a surprise appearance at the event, sporting a bright blue baseball cap and naturally attracting the attention of all of her classmates, who were so excited to see her again. It was a little overwhelming for her since her wounds were still healing. But she was back, and she had a big smile!

The students had planned a surprise, too. All of them wore T-shirts with Team Kerr lettering, and Kyra's second-grade classmates wore T-shirts that said Team Kyra. Their enthusiasm was a great boost to the spirits of our children. Even little Jaydalin, who wasn't even in school yet, jumped into the action, running and running around the gym with every group. Braylon took the prize for running the most laps, and his forty laps were an energetic expression of what it means to be Team Kerr. Since I couldn't be there like he had wished, Braylon did his best to run like crazy, just like I would have wanted. Jason, Grandpa Terry, and Grandma Kristine were there to share in all of the smiles.

Kyra's class demonstrated that they were on her team by giving her a hardbound book that they had compiled, a testament of people praying for her. As news about the accident went around on social media, people chimed in to say that they were praying, and each one mentioned where they lived. Eventually, there were people in all fifty states praying for Kyra and me! Kyra's second-grade schoolteacher took the lead to craft a book in which every state was represented by a picture in the sand, a leaf in a tree, or any other object in nature that forms the shape of a heart. It was a heartwarming reminder that people around the nation were with us in our crisis, crying out to God on our behalf.

That book provided our children with a visual image of what it means to pray for someone, even from as far away as Alaska or Hawaii. They got to see firsthand many people rallying with our family in a way that matters like nothing else. Months later, those life lessons still lingered in the minds of our children, and they now have a perspective to share with other children going through hard times. We recently asked all four of them what advice they would give to others their age, or anyone going through a similar tough experience. Their spontaneous responses say it all:

> If they believe in Christ, keep their faith in Him.
> Always pray and ask people to pray.
> Trust in God.
> Pray and trust in God.
> Do not worry, just focus on God and pray.
> Remember that God is in control.

Through all of the uncertainty at the hospital and even on the home front, our children found out what was solid and reliable. They grappled with the sadness and turmoil of what had happened, and they also found the joy of trusting God. Not to say that this was easy. From what I hear, while I was sleeping at the hospital, life at our house was somewhat chaotic for everyone. Even our dog, Moe, was confused! But the children—the entire family—all stuck together, and they held to their faith. My mother's pen carried their thoughts onto paper.

Mom's Journal
The Lord wants us to wait and trust! It is so hard! I know You can do all things, God, and I am trusting. But this is so hard!

My mother also noticed that I was slightly moving my right arm that day, which was an accomplishment. My left hand was reaching up toward my tracheostomy tube so much that the nurses put a glove on my hand to keep me from pulling on the tube unconsciously. As my mother described it, I was being feisty, like usual, even in the coma. But my zest for life hadn't pulled me out of that awfully long sleep—and that made it hard.

> **Mom's Journal**
> We need you to keep working your way back to us, babe! We miss you horribly. Nobody's life is the same without you here. We would never have chosen this walk, but God is using it Big-Time for His glory! And I know you are rejoicing in every person who gets saved because of this crazy thing that's happening. It's not over yet!

What she wrote in that last line was more correct than she even realized. The sequence of events on the morning of that dreadful accident had not yet been fully revealed, and soon I would know more clearly what this crazy calamity would mean for me and for many other people.

"Be still, and know that I am God" (Psalm 46:10). Those words seemed to swoop down from God in heaven to the heart of my mother on Saturday morning as she sat in the family room at the hospital in St. Paul. Having a spontaneous thought like this, as if it were a direct message from God, is not an everyday occurrence for my mother. It had come at just the right time. A shadow of despair was edging into her attitude, and this one sentence from the Psalms was the reassurance that she needed. *Be still.* There was no doubt that I was being still in the forced stillness of my coma. But was my mother being still, too? What mattered more than any physical restriction was remaining in the stillness of faith, remembering that God is God.

Already with that verse on her mind, as if God had deliberately tucked it into her thoughts, my mother picked up her devotional book to read and reflect. My father had been upstairs in my hospital room and joined her in the patients' family room for a few minutes. Reading a book was her normal practice, but today, it was different. She began to read out loud. *Be still, and know that I am God.* The first words on the page brought the exact message that she had already sensed in her heart. With this gripping thought, she was ready to sit back on yet another day of this seemingly endless vigil, knowing that God was carrying the story forward.

My mother logged in her journal the names of people who came to see me, although there were so many visitors that she didn't always keep track. Some of them were strangers to her, but it touched her heart to see the throng of supporters. After days of wearing a plain hospital gown, I was finally outfitted in some new pajamas. Of course, I was unaware of the change—all dressed up to keep sleeping. My friends came, even though I was asleep, and with a single sentence in her notes, my mother captured their sense of anticipation.

Mom's Journal
We are all waiting for your beautiful smile!

One of the visitors that day was Diane Ristau, who stopped by to drop off a plaque that a friend of hers had made. The beautifully painted lettering was simple and made a bold statement: *Be still, and know that I am God!*

The doctors removed the long, meandering trail of staples on my scalp that had sealed the wound where they had removed part of my skull, but they continued to offer little hope of further healing. One of the doctors brought my family into her office to discuss my prognosis. Turning to her computer, the doctor pulled up an illustration of a healthy brain as a point of comparison. Then she held up another image of a damaged brain, demonstrating the opposite extreme and saying to Jason, "This is where your wife is."

Standing up from her desk, the doctor started to talk in detail about the physical abilities that I would never regain. She stood next to the bookshelf in her office, making it an impromptu visual aid for the information that she was relaying. Pretending that the grid of shelves formed a graph, she said, "A fully functioning person is here, and your wife is here." The distance between those dots on her graph was a chasm. "She is not going to improve."

Jason felt lightheaded and walked out of the doctor's office. He couldn't bear to hear any more tough information like this. The doctor had spoken in a tone that was very matter-of-fact, and while Jason respected her position, he chose to persist in believing that God's healing power is a reality beyond the medical facts.

That night, Aunt Peggy called my mother, telling her something that clashed with the medical prognosis. The points on the graph that the doctor had formed on her wooden shelves were not nailed into place. They could move.

Mom's Journal
Peggy called and said in prayer the Lord told her the time was getting close and we were going to start seeing good things happen. . . . We are waiting and praising You, Lord!

It was Monday morning, three weeks after the accident. Kyra started going back to school for a few hours, easing into her activities gradually. Jason snapped a quick back-to-school photo of Kyra, standing tall with her colorful backpack on her shoulders, before she dashed out the door from the mudroom to the garage to get into the car. It felt as momentous as her first day of school, or even more, since she was a walking and running miracle.

The miracle was still happening. I wasn't ready to dash out the door anytime soon, but Aunt Peggy's words were right— good things were coming. I was still comatose, undergoing daily physical and occupational therapy sessions, which helped to keep my slumbering body limber.

My mother visited me in the family room after my therapy sessions that day, along with my friend Katie Moras. As my mother held my hand, Katie stood in front of me, eager to see some trace of the healing that everyone awaited. My mother noticed that my foot slid off the foot support on the wheelchair where I was sitting. Was that an intentional movement, or just gravity? She sat back, observing everything with Katie and later writing down what she had seen and heard.

Curious, Katie said, "Shannon, stretch your leg out." I did! I don't know how I did that, because I was oblivious to all of this.

Then Katie touched the side of my leg and told me to put it back up on the foot support of the wheelchair. I did!

Katie repeated that series of instructions and motions six times, and each time, according to my mother, I responded. Then Katie said, "Give me a thumbs-up." I did that too!

In an inexplicable way, I had sleepingly moved when Katie spoke. Because I was still completely unconscious, this wasn't the enormous breakthrough that would wrap up my hospital stay and send me home running victory laps. But it was a significant indication that my family was not foolish in their faith. My mother paused to register her impressions.

Mom's Journal

A lot of little things are starting to happen! This fits into what Peggy said last night—that we were going to start seeing good things happen. God is doing a work. We hear reports every day of how this whole thing is changing people's lives. So we keep walking one foot in front of the other and looking to Him to walk us through.

My parents joined Jason at the hospital at 11:30 a.m. and heard that in my therapy sessions I had been coached through some pedaling motions on a stationary bicycle. Stationary cycling was better than being stuck in a stagnant position, even if I couldn't move forward yet. There was still a lot of ground to cover. To keep propelling my progress, Jason read Scripture to me, and then my parents plunged into singing two tunes that I had known since my childhood. They started small, with "Two Little Eyes."

Two little eyes and golden hair,
Mommy's baby girl,
Asking the Lord His favorite prayer,
Mommy's baby girl.
She scrambles for sugar,
And upsets her tea,
Which you can never deny,
That nobody else is queen of the house,
Like mommy's baby girl.

It's a lighthearted little song by an unknown composer, and yet its lyrics seriously reinforced what my parents were hoping to see happen. When would my eyes and every part of me start performing like usual? Instead of sinking into deep thoughts about those unanswered questions, they launched into their second song, much sillier than the first. We don't know who wrote it, but the song had been part of our family for years. I had learned to sing about the Cannibal King long before I knew what it meant.

The Cannibal King with the brass nose ring
Fell in love with the dusty maiden

And every night in the pale moonlight
Across the lake he came

He hugged and he kissed his pretty little miss
In the shade of the bamboo tree
And every night in the pale moonlight
This is how it sounded to me-e-e

Ah-ump (kiss, kiss), ah-ump (kiss, kiss)
Ah-um, ditty-a-di-ada
Ah-ump (kiss, kiss), ah-ump (kiss, kiss)
Ah-um, ditty-a-di-ada
This is how it sounded to me-e-e

The song goes on and on, and they probably sang it with a giggle. This was not the last time that the playful song about the Cannibal King would fill the hospital room with a dose of laughter. My parents wondered how much I heard as I sat there not responding at all. My mother's jottings in her journal tell me that even though I was unconscious, my heart was still beating with life.

Mom's Journal

I was massaging your legs and feet, which you seem to enjoy! I can tell by your breathing and heart rate. I know you are coming back to us.

Underneath the surface of my sleep, I began to act very anxious, or so it seemed. My arms and legs were involuntarily moving a lot, while my heart rate was climbing to over 120 beats per minute. As my mother watched, my chest seemed to be working so hard to keep up with all the movement, and it broke her heart to watch my heart struggling.

My father observed my physical therapy session later that day, keeping a close eye on me while also glancing at the machines monitoring my vital signs. As my arms moved in a controlled, supervised exercise, my heart rate soared to 140, and my father told them to stop. For my parents, this phase of agitated movement was excruciatingly unfamiliar, and they didn't know if it was progress in the right direction. My mother waffled between anticipation and anguish as she wrote about the day's developments.

Mom's Journal
Today has been a harder day than just watching you moving, which is awesome! But what comes with that is your heart rate goes up, and I hate that part. It's hard because I don't know what you coming out of this is supposed to look like. I just want you awake and here.

Jason awoke with a sense of joy and strength. The peace that surpasses understanding had not slipped away, even after so many days of this uncertain ordeal. *I have this hope as an anchor for my soul*, he sang to himself as he listened to "Anchor" on the way to the hospital. *In everything I will trust in You.*

A family meeting with the Bethesda doctors later that day proved to be more encouraging than Jason had expected. The team evaluating my symptoms was pleased with how far I had come within the past week. My eyes were opening, and my limbs were unwittingly moving. I was still in a bizarre state of oblivion, but no one could label me as lifeless.

If I was ever going to walk on a stage in an auditorium and talk about my healing, a lot more needed to happen. Stepping one foot in front of the other to face a crowd of people was a distant prospect. But the doctors didn't discard the idea of healing as swiftly as they had in previous meetings. They started setting goals. One of them was for me to respond to commands with definite "yes" and "no" motions, other than squeezing a person's hand, which was merely a reflexive reaction. Another hurdle would be swallowing, an ability that had slipped away.

I also needed to keep sleeping, so the doctors said. In fact, they decided that I needed fewer people surrounding me so closely. My family took this rule seriously, while not quitting from their supportive stance by my side. My mother sifted through her thoughts in her journal, resisting the urge to hover constantly nearby because she knew that God was always at work.

Mom's Journal
They said we are there too much and they want you resting more and not to go in the room and try to stimulate you. We can go in but be quiet, pray, and don't talk or touch.

Lord, thank You for Your report of encouragement from the doctors today! We thank You and praise You for everything You are doing with Shannon and what You have done with the girls! By the authority given to us by Jesus, I again say to that mountain: move! Healing power in the name of Jesus! Thank You for Your healing and restoration. By Your stripes, she is healed!

FRIDAY
October 9, 2015

Some days were quieter, and rightly so. Jason started to hate Fridays because he would talk with people who were on the brink of the weekend, gearing up for activities that were both exciting and mundane. Everything was so apparently normal for our friends. For Jason, normality did not exist anymore, and the weekend was always unpredictable. He couldn't make any plans because his new normal was a front-row seat in the hospital room of a brain trauma patient—his own wife—watching what God would do with my life.

In staying nearby to watch over me, Jason's Fridays were quite extraordinary. Not everyone gets to ponder the mysteries of a real-life angel, like he got to do during the slow hours of silence, and as Jason sat by my bed, God was showing him a miracle in the making.

Mom's Journal
Miracles work.

My mother's brief notes in her journal were a booming drumbeat, a percussive accompaniment to a quiet miracle that was unfolding before the eyes of anyone who would look closely enough to see it.

The weekends were long for Jason and for the children, back at home in Lakeville. Home was a big, empty house without Mom there. Sometimes they even slept in the same room, finding comfort in being together. Jason never quite knew where he would find Braylon in the mornings. Often, our youngest boy would get up during the night and nest with a blanket in one of the corners of the house. Tucked into a makeshift hideout to sleep, Braylon wished I were the one to call his name softly, waking him up in the morning like I had when I left the house the last time. It was tough, but every day they got up and kept active.

A steadfast father and husband, Jason rallied our household in between his visits to the hospital, and on Saturday he showed me a photograph of our four children. My eyes were open but only staring blankly, so he didn't expect me to react. But I did seem to look at each of the children in the picture, my eyes following as I gazed at Trenton, Braylon, Kyra, and Jaydalin. Even in my faint stare, I'm sure that deep down I missed them as much as they missed me.

My mother knew how the children felt. She helped care for them on the home front whenever she wasn't at the hospital, taking note as they navigated this uncomfortable, strange scene.

Mom's Journal

Jayda asked me the other day if I would be her mommy until her mommy got home. It broke my heart. I told her, "Honey, I will be whatever you want me to be."

Before closing her journal that night, my mother cried out to God, longing to see me be able to swallow. Without swallowing and speaking, how could I ever be a voice to the nations, like Liz had said? So far I couldn't even speak to my children.

Today, my parents went to church instead of going to the hospital, which turned out to be more emotional than they anticipated. The hugs and words of encouragement were a much-needed refreshment from the harsh reality of the crisis they were enduring. One of the songs in church was especially meaningful to my mother.

> **Mom's Journal**
> We sang a song, "Prince of Peace," and I sang it out with tears streaming down my face for you, Marie!

When my mother calls me by my middle name, there is a tender heart-to-heart connection that only a mother and daughter share. Jason sent her a picture that he had taken of me at the hospital and reported that my heart rate was steady. The calmness of my pulse was a relief after the agitation of previous days, as if the Prince of Peace were working to settle the wind shear in the storm.

It was another Monday. Things at home shifted gears slightly as Terry and Kristine, Jason's parents, returned to Michigan. With one pair of doting grandparents out of town again, my mother took on even more of my responsibilities, picking up the boys from school regularly and being a warm presence at the house. This meant that she couldn't visit me as often.

Also, it was Jaydalin's first day of preschool, which started with a field trip to a local apple orchard. It was a bright beginning to her school career, and Grandma Shelly captured a photo of Jaydalin's bright grin as she sat on a huge pumpkin at the orchard. At a glance, no one would know that the happy little four-year-old in the puffy, pink-trimmed jacket and fuzzy pink hat had been through such a terribly dramatic event just one month ago.

At the hospital, the pace was slower. The doctors performed a CT scan of my brain to determine if they could replace the section of my skull that had been surgically removed on the day of the accident. They discovered that there was still so much swelling and bruising that it would be another two weeks before the procedure might be possible.

This slow-motion miracle was not moving at a tempo that we would have wished, but the momentum of prayer kept pressing forward. Kristi Hedstrom continued to post updates and prayer requests on the CaringBridge® site, and with each post came another word from the Scriptures.

> "I remain confident of this:
>> I will see the goodness of the LORD
>> in the land of the living.
>
> Wait for the LORD;
>> be strong and take heart
>> and wait for the LORD" (Psalm 27:13–14).

The day began promptly at 7:30 a.m., not as an emergency but in an attempt to avoid one. As a deliberative precaution, I was shuttled one mile down the road to St. Joseph's Hospital, where they surgically implanted an inferior vena cava (IVC) filter in my abdomen to prevent blood clots from causing a pulmonary embolism. The doctors at Bethesda had been administering blood-thinning medication, which was causing the opening of my tracheostomy to bleed, and this IVC filter procedure was a corrective measure. Thankfully, the doctors were attentive to my condition, and their proactive medical care guarded my lungs from any blood-induced blockage.

This was not the type of instant healing that my family longed to see. And while they waited for that healing to come from God's hands, people around the world continued to pray, tracking along with the bullet points in the CaringBridge® posts. A friend of ours who lives in the Middle East sent a very encouraging text message to Jason, saying that as he prayed, he felt an extreme peace and confidence in my healing. My mother, too, received a positive text message.

Mom's Journal

This morning Stephanie sent me a text that said a pastor she knows has been following the CaringBridge® site, and he is praying for her brain to heal and for her to wake up. "I felt God say it would happen in His timetable. As I've watched her progress from afar the last few weeks, I believe this most certainly will come true! God is with her, and He is at work in Shannon's situation. I can't even imagine all that we are learning and will learn about God through this whole time. I will continue to join you all in praying for her as she recovers." Sounds like confirmation and the Lord once again saying it's going to be OK. Thank You, Lord, for Your words of reassurance.

Messages like this inspired my family in their faith and in their daily activities. My mother was busy filling in for me, making sure the children finished their homework before Jason returned from visiting me at the hospital. She wanted to be sure that they had free time with their father, and her motherly heart glowed on the pages of her journal that day.

Mom's Journal
You have great kiddos. Shannon Marie, you guys have done a great job raising them.

It was day thirty, one month since the accident. After so many prayers, would this be the day of my healing?

No one anticipated that the one-month mark would bring another crisis, one that I would narrowly survive. The IVC filter could prevent a pulmonary embolism, but there was a different problem now. We were back to dealing with the basics—I was having trouble breathing. My lungs became so badly congested that the doctors X-rayed my chest and discovered that I had pneumonia. They prescribed antibiotics and decided that I was still able to proceed with my regular physical therapy session. My breathing was labored, though, and occasionally they would suction the phlegm from my tracheostomy tube.

Jason was at the hospital that morning, as usual, and was conversing with the therapists before my routine therapy appointment. My room was on the fourth floor in the brain injury unit, and Jason began to push me in a wheelchair toward the elevator to ride downstairs to the second floor, where the therapy activity area is located. The therapists followed along with Jason and me, and they continued to chat in the elevator while I sat there in my unresponsive state. Jason couldn't see my face since I was in front of him in the wheelchair, but he had grown oddly accustomed to my quietness.

Once Jason reached the activity area, he stopped for the therapists to take over with my routine movement session. Then they looked. The therapists who were walking along with Jason glanced at my face—it was blue. They panicked! Everyone suddenly realized that I was suffocating. The pneumonia was worse than anyone had realized, and my tracheostomy tube was clogged. My attempts to gasp for breath were futile.

It was Code Blue. A hospital staff member nearby pushed the emergency announcement button, and about thirty people came from all over the building in response to the alarm. The doctors and nurses were questioning among themselves what was happening. Is this a heart attack? A stroke? That very morning, they had determined that I was stable, with no indication that the pneumonia was so severe. Yet, in that moment, I was closer to death, and panic homed in on the picture.

Lord, how can You bring me to this point? Jason thought. *After all that we've faced in this past month, now my wife is a Code Blue case, suffocating?* The surrounding people seemed paralyzed, unsure what to do. So Jason spoke.

"You need to suction her," Jason said urgently.

Acting quickly on Jason's firm order, the doctors suctioned my tracheostomy tube.

I coughed. And I coughed some more. I had air in my lungs again, and I was breathing. This was an enormous relief to everyone gathered around me, and yet the hospital staff was nervous. The specialty at this medical facility was not intensive care, and the attending doctor who stood next to Jason seemed frantic, concerned about what to do next. The doctor didn't want anyone dying on his watch. Neither did Jason.

In that instant, Jason realized that he had a choice to make. It would be natural to have hard feelings and make a loud scene, scolding the hospital staff for what had turned into a life-threatening episode. But Jason tossed those thoughts aside, remembering that he was not only a husband but also a representative of Jesus, his Savior.

"Listen, this is what happened . . ." Jason said to the doctor. With calm strength, he explained my condition in more detail and my need for closer supervision. Jason's words were direct, but spoken as a peacemaker. As a result, the doctors moved me from the brain injury unit to the sixth-floor respiratory care unit. I had nurses with me around the clock, and with their constant attention, I recovered from the incident.

But it had been a terrible scare for Jason. It was hard for him to fall asleep that night after looking at my terrifying blue face. God had not left me unattended, though, and the unfolding miracle had not ended.

THURSDAY
October 15, 2015

While monitoring my respiratory issues, the doctors at Bethesda Hospital decided that something in my lung was aggravating my situation. Apparently, a chipped tooth or dental filling had dislodged into my lung upon the impact of the collision. They told my family that they planned to take me to St. Joseph's Hospital down the street again in a few days, this time to surgically remove the foreign object in my lung.

This was turning into a week of one complication after another, not the rapid progress that my mother or anyone else wanted to see. But my mother held onto God as she continued to track the ordeal in her journal.

Mom's Journal
They are going to go in and try to remove the tooth or filling at the beginning of next week. I am not excited about this at all, but if it clears up your lungs and you can move forward, then I guess let's get it done. Kids are doing great. You can really tell the Lord is holding them.

Jason and I spent our sixteenth wedding anniversary in full obedience to our marriage vow, which declares that we would be together in love for better or for worse. It would have been a storybook moment if I had woken up for the occasion, but I didn't. And yet our love had not diminished on this disappointing day, because when we fell in love, it was for life. As Jason sat by my bedside, looking into my seemingly empty eyes, the question that I had asked him in the moment when we met was still arresting his attention. *Who do you believe in?* And his answer was still the same. *I believe in Jesus.*

It was a bittersweet day for Jason at the hospital. He still believed in Jesus, and he still believed that I would be healed. Healing in my body and brain was one thing—what Jason wondered was if I would remember him. He was concerned that I might think he was nothing more than a kind stranger, like any other visitor treating me with gentle care by my bedside. Would I recognize Jason as my husband, the man I loved? He would have to wait for that answer, while loving me on this day, our anniversary, and onward.

My mother kept the children content at home with puzzles and hot chocolate on a cold afternoon, apologizing in her journal for splurging on marshmallows to top off the hot chocolate. More artificial food in my absence! Then she added a tenderhearted comment.

Mom's Journal
Shannon, your dad has been amazing through this. He spends most of every day and evening with you. We both did till the Kerrs left, but Dad is right with you, making sure you are OK. Jay too. The men in your life love you so much. We need you to wake up, my honey girl!!

On Saturday, Jason stayed with me at the hospital most of the day while my mother stayed at our house with the children. Her sense of longing seeps through the pages of her journal.

> **Mom's Journal**
> It was a beautiful day so we were outside a lot. I love sitting on your red chairs on your porch, imagining you sitting there doing your devotions.

That day would come, when I would sit on my red chair in front of our house, reflecting on that one unforgettable trip down the driveway, and it would be more meaningful than my mother even imagined. But all that she knew was this present day, sitting in my place as a mother to my children and praying for an unknown future day when I would come home again.

> **Mom's Journal**
> When I am out and about and I see moms with their kids, it makes me so sad! I am doing my best and the Lord is holding them, but I am not you. But I thank the Lord He is holding you and keeping you safe.

I had been restless for several days. My jolting, uncontrolled movements were disconcerting to watch, and they were dangerous, a risk for accidental injury. The doctors said that my comatose motions were a typical phase of the recovery process, but they gave me sleep-inducing medications to relax my body. I wore the infamous helmet a lot, protecting my head from banging against the side of the bed.

On Sunday, I seemed to settle into a more restful mode. It was a fitting interlude for Kristi's post on the CaringBridge® site. Jason had suggested that she pause from the regular updates to focus on how God had been answering specific prayer requests so far. So Kristi scrolled back through the concerns ever since the day of the accident and crafted a long list of positive developments. It was a very tangible testament to the power of prayer and, ultimately, to the power of God.

As he had been saying all along, Jason wanted people to pray. When people would sympathetically tell him, "My thoughts are with you," Jason's reaction was that this was pointless. He didn't want them to think; he wanted them to pray. The list of answered prayers was Jason's way of saying, "Keep them coming, keep them coming!"

Sunday had been a soothing day of rest, but overnight it was the opposite. The nurses watching me during the night shift in the respiratory unit said that I was restless for all but twenty minutes. They told my mother that they had gone through two bottles of lotion massaging me, trying to help me relax. If only I would use that energy to wake up!

Every day seemed to bring a new twist or turn. The St. Joseph's Hospital doctors performed a CT scan to check on the tooth particle in my lung and determined that it was too deeply imbedded to be removed safely. They concluded that it was less risky to just let it remain, confirming an original decision that the doctors at Hennepin County Medical Center had made. My family had worried about the surgical procedure in the first place, and now they were only partially relieved. Hopefully the fragment trapped in my lung wouldn't trigger more complications with my breathing.

It was truly a journey through unfamiliar territory for my family as they trusted in God, knowing that He would be faithful to care for me. And as Jason had asked, the prayers kept coming.

At 5:15 p.m., my brother Dan was driving home from work, praying as he headed north into the clear late-afternoon sky in Chippewa Falls, Wisconsin. With all the ups and downs of my medical status, he had been hearing people say that the idea of my healing was a false mirage. So Dan was begging God to please —please—heal his big sister.

Then he looked toward the northeast, where something caught his eye. Along the skyline, a rainbow appeared in the sky. It was a day with no sun and no rain, and the colors streaked across the horizon as if God had taken a paintbrush and swiped a message in the air, reminding Dan of His promise to preserve life. This was the second time that Dan had experienced something like this. Dan and his wife, Beth, had seen a double rainbow as a promise from God before the birth of their twin daughters.

Arriving home, Dan rushed inside. "Shannon's going to be fine," he said to Beth. "There was a rainbow." Dan was so stunned that this was all he could say. He ran outside onto the deck of their house, and Beth followed close behind him, looking up at the sky as he pointed at the rainbow.

"That's so cool!" Beth exclaimed. "But there's no rain." It was unique, unlike any rainbow that would usually burst forth from the clouds after a downpour. There was no doubt in Dan's mind that his confidence in God's promise was not a freakish hallucination. God would heal me.

Dan called my mother to tell her what he had seen. Hearing his excitement, she recalled that this was now the third rainbow appearance since the accident. The first had been the one that April had seen on her way to the hospital, within several hours of the crash. Then, my mother recounted how she had seen a rainbow on the wall in the family area on the fourth floor at Bethesda. It was a prism-like rainbow, projected into the room as light streamed through the window, and it had reassured her of God's presence in the darkness of the hospital. My mother joined Dan in his enthusiasm and in embracing the message of promise that each rainbow conveyed.

Dan was still thinking about the rainbow sighting as he watched the ten o'clock news that night. As the news program drew to a close, the weather reporter commented on the rainbow that had appeared in the sky that afternoon. "There really was no reason for it," the meteorologist stated. He went on to discuss how certain atmospheric conditions can create a clash of crystals that form a rainbow in cold weather. But it had been a summery day. The meteorologist concluded, "There is no explanation for why this rainbow happened today."

"It's mine!" Dan chimed in, talking back to the television. The rainbow in the sky was his to claim, his to remember, as a gift from God.

There was a glimmer of progress the day after the rainbow. Not that I was waking up, but at least some of the surrounding circumstances were improving. The pneumonia was gone, so the doctors took away the IV antibiotic bag that was providing my medication. And my breathing had stabilized so much that they also inserted a speaking valve on the outside of my tracheostomy tube. Of course, this was just a preparatory measure because I was not even conscious, let alone talking. The intention was to facilitate my breathing, allowing me to breathe more through my nose, and to create the conditions so that eventually I could swallow.

My mother kept logging in her journal the names of my visitors at the hospital, based on what my father told her, and she recorded what was happening on the home front. Braylon was doing his homework . . . Jaydalin had a head cold . . . and my mother was doing everyone's laundry.

Mom's Journal
Dad said you were much calmer today, which we like to see. We hate seeing you agitated. But maybe agitation is a good thing. We just don't know. The Lord knows.

Mom's Journal

Today was a little discouraging because nothing changed, and we so desperately want to see change every day! Forgive me, Lord, for grumbling. I thank You and praise You for the miracles You have given us!

My mother's discouragement about my stagnant coma was brightened by the fact that Kyra was bouncing back tremendously, a true miracle full of life. Jason and Kyra shot basketballs together, and between dribbling and rebounding, Kyra scored twenty-five baskets! Her reflexes were great, and mine were gradually reviving in tiny strides. Although nothing had changed because I was still unconscious, I did score one point. Jason held his cell phone in front of my face at my bedside and played a video of Braylon, Kyra, and Jaydalin singing for me. Jason noticed that I seemed to watch the video intently, and I even reached out to touch a corner of the cell phone. Apparently there was something happening in my brain, even if only a reflexive motion.

Not so fast! The hospital staff conducted a test and determined that I still needed to rely on my tracheostomy tube more than they had realized. Reaching the milestone of swallowing would have to wait because basic breathing was the priority of the day. They reactivated the tracheostomy tube, and the nurses settled in to gauge the outcome.

However, my physical abilities were edging in the right direction. Brenda, my occupational therapist, had performed a test on October 2 to evaluate my responsiveness. I had scored a meager 8 out of a possible 111 points. Today, she tested me again, and this time I attained a score of 32. It was still a long distance from the finish line of 111, but it was better than regressing. My mother's positivity shone when she commented that I had quadrupled my results in less than three weeks.

In physical therapy, I was assisted to stand upright with support, allowing my feet to be flat on the floor. My tendons were tight, my flexibility as an athlete stretched to the limit. If I were going to run again, I would need to keep fighting. And I would need to hear in my spirit the lyrics of my favorite song, propelling me to press forward. *Take me deeper than my feet could ever wander, and my faith will be made stronger in the presence of my Savior.*

And yet my family would face yet another reversal before the day ended. My mother heard the report from my father when he returned from the hospital.

Mom's Journal
When Dad got home, he told me a new doctor said he wants that tooth or filling out and he is going to try tomorrow morning. This news kind of did me in. Dad says the doctor said it's no big deal to go down your trach and retrieve it. We

had two other doctors say leave it, so I pray if they do it, it goes well and the Lord is the one who sent this new doctor. I rebuke anything that will bring harm to you.

FRIDAY
October 23, 2015

Jason persisted in his certainty that I would be healed, despite all the detours that kept popping up along the road to recovery. He did have a hesitation, though. He felt uneasy about the prospect of the procedure to remove the foreign particle from my lung, and early in the afternoon on Friday, Jason shared his thoughts with my mother.

The minor surgery had been scheduled for 10:00 a.m. that morning, but the new doctor had gotten mixed up about the arrangements for the anesthesia. Since there was no anesthesiologist available, the doctor ordered another drug and rescheduled the appointment for later that afternoon. At the end of the day, writing in her journal, my mother described in detail what happened.

> **Mom's Journal**
> Jason said he just didn't know what to think of your new doctor who was going to do the procedure on you. He said he changed how they were putting you out (using a local instead of putting you out, doing it in your room instead of sending you over to St. Joseph's Hospital). I called Dad up and said, "Don't let them touch our daughter." Dad called Jason again, and he canceled the procedure. Two other doctors had said to leave it and scar tissue would form around it. So this was a completely different thinking that came out of nowhere.

It was a hard call to make, canceling the procedure at Bethesda. The doctors had already canceled it earlier in the week, choosing not to risk it on Monday, and then this new doctor had announced that he wanted to go ahead with it on Friday. My family felt unsure about the new doctor's recommendation, and they asked him not to proceed. God confirmed the decision, providing another evidence that the prayers of the people supporting our family were effective. My mother jotted in her journal what she heard from my brother Dan.

Mom's Journal

This is our God thing for the day. Dan's church staff had been putting a lot of prayer into this week and sent Dan a text when they saw him post that the procedure had been canceled. Here is a text from Dan. Confirms what we did was correct according to the Lord. "Hey Dan, it's Pastor Allison. So I have to tell you this crazy God story about Shannon's surgery. On Tuesday morning in staff prayer time we prayed for her, and I specifically prayed for the pneumonia to be gone immediately and surgery for the filling in her lung to be canceled. I prayed that the filling would disappear and she would not have to undergo another surgery on Wednesday morning. We saw the post answering this prayer and were thrilled! I knew God had given me the exact words to pray, and I knew He had taken care of it! So today when I saw surgery was back on, I prayed and told God that I knew He had this taken care of and that the surgery needed to be canceled again."

After the doctors left my room, a head RN spoke with my father, saying that she was not comfortable with the procedure at all and that my family had been right in advocating against the idea. Far away in Wisconsin, people were praying, and God guided the day's events, protecting me in that moment of decision. This is what God had been doing all along, and soon I would understand even more about how He had done this when the angel sat next to me in the front seat of our van.

The coma was so perplexing. I was still asleep, totally unaware of anything in my surroundings, and I don't remember even a little bit of what took place. Oddly enough, my movements were increasing in tiny increments. How I could do any of this while unconscious, that I don't know.

Brenda, my occupational therapist, documented what happened in my therapy session when she asked me to shake my head "no." She watched as I responded by moving my eyes back and forth. I have no idea what I was thinking because I remember nothing. When Brenda asked me to give her a reaction to signify "yes," I feebly formed a partial thumbs-up. When my therapist lightly tossed a ball to me, she noted that I was able to catch it, though maybe that was more about the laws of gravity causing it to fall into my arms than about any skill from my past basketball career.

At least I was moving a little bit, according to the people watching me, even if I was somnolent. What moved my father's heart was when I extended my arms toward him. I was unaware, but my movement in his direction impacted him as if it had been intentional. He was still longing for the day when I could actually give him a hug.

After church on Sunday, Jason and my parents took the children to eat at Jimmy John's. We not only own several Jimmy John's restaurants, we also really like their sandwiches! This was our normal routine, except that normality had become blurry.

In the afternoon, Jason took Trenton and Braylon to the hospital to visit me while my parents went back to our house with the girls. It still seemed premature for the girls to see me unconscious and to look into my blank stare. Although Kyra and Jaydalin had been in the accident with me, they hadn't visited me at Hennepin County Medical Center or at Bethesda Hospital. They were so young, and this calamity was such a heavy topic.

But the boys had already confronted the reality, and this was to be just another visit. Apparently, it was too much for Braylon. Late that night, upstairs in his bedroom, Braylon burst into an anguished wail. It was a loud, gut-wrenching cry, and Jason rushed to his side. What Braylon needed was consolation, and between sobs he told Jason how he had felt at the hospital.

My inability to recognize my own son had an agonizing effect on him. Braylon said that he could be anybody, standing by my bedside, and I wouldn't know the difference. Jason comforted him, understanding that our brave little coyote-hunting boy, who likes to go out into the woods to push dead trees over just for the fun of it, was needing a gentle hug and the soft words of a father's love. It would be a while before I could do the same for him as his mother.

After the emotional outbreak of the night before, Jason let the children sleep in on Monday morning, and they left for school after 9:30 a.m. At the same time, I wasn't relaxing well at all, and my restlessness was an ongoing strain on my brain as well as my body.

Feeble as I was, I was at least unwittingly able to physically move some parts of my body. Jason attended my physical therapy session, where they had me up on my feet, retraining my limbs in a walking motion. Something that had once been so familiar was now so strange, as if walking were a foreign concept for my brain. With my therapist supporting my right side, which was the weakest, and Jason holding me on my left side, I shuffled forward about ten yards. Jason filled my mother in on the day's feat, which seemed ridiculously small compared to my 100-meter sprints, but it was better than nothing, and she jotted her impressions.

> **Mom's Journal**
>
> We are thanking the Lord for every little thing we see! We are praying always and continually. I wake up on and off all night, and I am praying big-time for God to move this mountain and have you up and back to normal. We are standing on Your promises, Lord!

Jason's parents, Terry and Kristine, came back into town to help my parents in caring for our children. Before settling into their role as grandparents, they drove straight to Bethesda Hospital. It had been more than two weeks since they had returned to Michigan, and they were eager to observe firsthand how I had changed or progressed.

When they arrived at the hospital, I was downstairs in a therapy session. Although the nurses were reluctant to interrupt my session, they sensed the earnestness in Terry and Kristine's request to see me right away. As Terry and Kristine entered the activity room, where many other patients were also being treated, they approached me and saw me look up, stopping what I was doing. They looked at me, and I gazed back at them.

Was I looking at Terry and Kristine merely because they had been a distraction, or had I actually recognized them? As they stayed longer, they realized that my gaze was still empty. My eyes would look at them, but it was as if there was nothing happening inside. And yet that instant when my reflexive response was centered on them was momentous in a small way. It assured them that I had not gotten worse during their absence. If anything, I was getting a little bit better.

The doctors told my family that today could be a turning point, or it could not. The swelling on my brain had reduced enough that it was time to go to Hennepin County Medical Center for neurosurgery to replace the piece of my skull that they had urgently removed on the day of the accident.

There was no way to predict the results. It was possible that I would stay the same, submerged in the fog of the coma, but it was also possible that I would begin to improve more rapidly. According to their medical expertise, the neurosurgery team acknowledged that there was potential for transformative progress, as my brain would feel more protected and secure once my skull was back where it belonged. But there were no assurances.

The surgery was successful, as they attached the segment of my skull into place with four titanium plates. The nurses informed Jason that I was at Level II on the Rancho Scale of Cognitive Functioning, which charts the phases of consciousness of a person recovering from traumatic brain injury and post-coma trauma. At Cognitive Level I, there is no response at all, and now I was at the second level, which corresponds to a minimal, generalized response. There were still other quadrants on the scale ahead of me, and even the following two levels were grim. The chart also prescribed the best methods of interaction to aid my recovery, and at this stage I needed a lot of quiet rest.

As I came out of the surgery in the post-operative room, the nurses let Jason and my father stop by briefly. The atmosphere was very restrictive to prevent any disturbances after such a massive, fragile surgery, and they were not allowed to linger long. As they started to walk away from my bedside and out into the hallway, the nurse came running.

"Jason!" the nurse called out. "I think you need to come stay with your wife because she has really responded to your voice."

I was still asleep, but my agitated reaction, extending my arms as if I were reaching out to him, sent a surge of renewed hope through Jason. *I am healed, I know I am.* Jason had never stopped believing the lyrics of the song recording from the Friday night after the accident. I had survived the surgery, and there was hope on the horizon. Jason knew that God would heal me. My reaction to Jason's voice reassured him that there was a deep level of recognition within me. The healing was happening, and maybe his yearning would soon be fulfilled. Maybe soon I would be able to express my awareness that Jason is my husband, the man I love.

THURSDAY
October 29, 2015

I spent the night at Hennepin County Medical Center, restless throughout the dark overnight hours, closely monitored by the nurses. Jason visited in the morning, and in the afternoon he went for a long walk in the woods near our house, waiting for me to wake up, waiting to see what God would do next.

Someone else called my mother, telling her that they had a strong sense that I would eventually be standing in front of large groups of women, sharing my testimony of healing. My mother had started counting these divine visions, and this was now the fourth, all of them confirming that one day I would walk . . . and speak . . . and have a story to tell.

I wasn't there yet, but I was making progress in recovering smoothly from the surgery at Hennepin County Medical Center. In the afternoon, I was shuttled back to Bethesda Hospital, returning to the brain injury unit on the fourth floor. As the doctors had suspected, the mending of my skull was producing desirable results, and my abilities and awareness were already starting to improve.

Jason observed that 98 percent of my movements seemed intentional, as if my brain was thinking about my motions, not just reacting compulsively. This was his assessment, while I have no recollection of anything—0 percent. When getting ready to stand, I scooted forward in my chair and looked at my feet. And when Jason passed me a cloth to wipe my mouth, I took it from his hand and raised it to my face. The increments were small but identifiable. Also, I was coughing with more force, which was positive because it meant that the nurses didn't have to suction the phlegm out of my mouth quite as much.

One episode in particular seemed to give the most evidence that not only was my skull recovering from the surgery, but also my mind was alive within the confines of my comatose brain trauma. Jason was with me in the hospital room when it happened and remembers it well. I don't remember it at all. He asked me for a kiss, not knowing what my reaction would be. To his surprise, I leaned forward and slightly puckered my lips! The complex

Rancho Scale of Cognitive Functioning had said nothing about when to expect a kiss! Was this just a figment of his imagination, a fairytale about Prince Charming kissing a damsel in distress?

Even my mother heard about the little kiss, the slightest display of spunk that lifted the atmosphere a little bit on Friday night. The next day, another message confirmed again that the cloud of despair was indeed going to lift.

Mom's Journal

Jennifer Gordon is a gal who brought her husband and daughter up to see us at Bethesda. They don't know you but have some of the same friends, and she is from Owatonna. She sent a card to us and said while she was praying, SHE WILL RUN went through her mind in capital letters! And she knew it was God.

My mother also knew it was God, especially since the woman who passed along that all-caps message didn't even know that I am a runner. The message was clear: fast or slow, I would keep racing forward.

SUNDAY
November 1, 2015

It was another Sunday, another weekend away from home in Lakeville, away from my family. "How's Mom? How's Mom? How's Mom?" the girls had been asking every day. They wanted to see me, but Jason was wary of frightening them with the sight.

Today he felt that the time had come. Two nurses from our church community met Jason and the children on the fourth floor of the hospital in the family meeting area to informally counsel the girls and ease them into the experience. They told Kyra and Jaydalin that my hair was shaved short against my scalp and that I had a tube sticking out of my neck. Then they showed photos of me, starting from the back of my head as I sat in a wheelchair and circling around toward a front view.

Most importantly, the nurses warned the girls that I might not recognize them at all. The adults in the room watched warily as the girls approached me. Kyra, who is a natural bundle of joy, was undeterred and put her arm around me before even pausing to look too closely, while Jaydalin lagged behind, startled by my shuddering cough. The nurses had been right; I only stared blankly, like usual.

Jason watched the entire scene and saw how scary it was for his little girls as the reality of my condition sunk in for them. Besides the empty look in my eyes, what bothered Kyra and Jaydalin the most was my hair—my flowing hair that was gone. But Kyra, young as she was at age seven, did something that astonished all of the teary-eyed adults gathered around the sad reunion. Noticing the small chalkboard propped up in my room, Kyra picked up a piece of white chalk and with the precise printing of a second-grader, wrote: *The LORD himself will fight for you. Just stay calm. Exodus 14:14.*

It was all so strange. I was unaware of my own girls, not remembering even the slightest glimpse of their visit. And yet, in my therapy session, I grabbed a pencil and held it correctly, as if poised to write. I couldn't even say hello, but apparently I had something to say, getting so much closer to being able to write my story!

So far, though, everything was one long nap as I responded increasingly to stimuli and expanded my repertoire of mobility. It was as if I were sleepwalking, moving in a dreamlike state, except that it was still an odd nightmare. Or maybe it was more like a writer suffering from writer's block, caught in a creative slowdown where thoughts are murky shadows, while on the brink of an inspiration.

In the morning, Jason took me outside in a wheelchair, giving me my first breath of fresh air since the accident. He noticed that I seemed to relax and bask in being beyond the rigid walls of the hospital and back in the world where the sky was as clear and blue as the last time I'd seen it.

Orange-hued dry leaves covered the ground and speckled the paved pathway, crinkling underneath the tires of the wheelchair as we quietly inched ahead, just as we'd been doing inside the dreaded hospital for weeks. As we turned along the corners of the path, the sun beaming in our eyes, I made no mental connection to the blinding rays of sunshine on the morning of my fateful drive eastward into the sunrise. I had no recollection of that moment in the past, only the fleeting present enjoyment of being outdoors. When we went inside, I didn't remember the wheelchair stroll, but I was always ready for more. My father took me out again in the afternoon, gently pushing me forward, edging toward the horizon that I needed to keep exploring.

When my mother wrote in her journal on Wednesday, it was as if she had been along on Tuesday's outings with Jason and my father. Instead, it was her endless motherly encouragement and her persistent prayers that were helping to prod me forward.

Mom's Journal

You are continuing to progress, Shannon Marie. You are moving forward every day! Dad and Jason are very pleased. We are so blessed by your progress. You want to get up and walk and sit, and I know you are thinking, *I have to get going here, I have things to do so I can get out of here!* We just continue to pray and believe in your healing!

The wheelchair was not my only mode of transportation. I was walking, even if it was only in short increments and with support. My mother knew that walking was only an intermediate phase because she had watched me grow up and was sure that she would see me run again, just like when I was a little girl.

Mom's Journal

I remember the card Jennifer Gordon sent. The Lord gave her in prayer the words in capital letters: SHE WILL RUN. It just spoke to me. I knew her message was God-given, but this morning it dawned on me how perfect and personal it actually was because she doesn't know you to know that that is who you are and always have been. You RUN! Jason brought your cool tennis shoes up to you, and they put them on you and you were walking behind a walker. The therapist had to help with your right side by pushing your foot forward. But you are up and moving. She said it's your starting point to running.

It was a day like any other, as far as I knew. That is to say, I don't remember anything, but for my mother it was an amazing day. From my mother's perspective, the Shannon she loved was on the brink of truly coming back to her.

On Friday evening, my mother visited me at Bethesda Hospital, kneeling on the floor in front of my chair and looking at my face, where my expression was disturbingly aloof. It was so difficult for her to confront my dull demeanor, which was such a stark contrast to the spunky daughter she had raised. She gazed at my eyes, recalling that we are in the brown-eyed club, as Jaydalin calls us. We are three generations and three pairs of brown eyes, bubbling with gusto. Except that my gusto was gone. My mother's heart welled up with emotion as she sat there looking at me, and that night she wrote in her journal what happened next.

Mom's Journal

I told you we were in the brown-eyed club. You put your head down to my forehead. We were cheek to cheek. You were pulling me in. It was so awesome. I needed that so much. I was crying. I always sing "Two Little Eyes" and "The Cannibal King" to you. You had your talking trach in, and you would make sounds and your lips would move, so you're trying, sweetheart. That's one thing about you. You always push hard to complete the goal.

In the instant when we were cheek to cheek, my mother felt like I knew her. Because I don't have any memory of this at all, I can't say for sure what was happening in my mind. I was still in a phase where my brain trauma clouded all of my perceptions, and I was unaware of anything. But I was able to instinctively respond to sounds. And regardless of how damaged my brain still was, I like to think that in the depths of my heart, there was a mother-daughter connection in that moment.

That same evening, my mother paused to take a picture of me, along with two of my friends who were visiting. Stephanie Balvin, who came to the hospital a lot, was there with Melissa McKernon, who had flown in from California to see me. As my mother snapped the shot of the three of us, she noticed that I seemed to attempt a feeble smile for the camera. She was amazed because it was the first semblance of a smile that she had seen on my face in nearly two months. After so many weeks of wondering when God would heal me, finally my mother's spirit was smiling at the sight of these developments. Healing seemed to be nearer than ever to her line of vision, and as she wrote that night, she seemed to be confident that my lifelong gusto was back, too.

Mom's Journal
You are doing so many small things that just show us you are coming back and you are working so hard to get there.

My family was off and running, with sports tournaments and a quick stop for frozen custard on a busy autumn Saturday. At the hospital, the holding pattern was still the order of the day, until a breakthrough in the healing of my brain would put me back in the game again. The only difference was that now the agonizing vigil had taken on an atmosphere of increased anticipation, as my mother described.

Mom's Journal
Dad headed up to be with you around 11:00 a.m. I keep thinking about you and wondering what you are getting figured out today.

THE COMPREHENSION
November 8, 2015 through December 9, 2015

It had been a while since any of the phenomenal encounters that had caused hope to swell anew during the darkest days of my coma. Was that because the skies were now brightening? Maybe my family didn't need another angel to reassure them that God was caring for me. Already, they were starting to see small glimmers of the healing that they knew would come. When circumstances had seemed the bleakest, God kept restoring their confidence, sending them messages that spurred their faith.

Faith was gradually becoming sight. But what about that fourth person in the van—the angel that no one had yet been able to explain? Surely there must be some spiritual meaning behind that extraordinary sight from day one. What remained to be seen was what would happen first—a breakthrough in my healing, or a breakthrough in understanding the purpose of that inexplicable angel appearance.

I was not yet healed in my brain and body. My recovery was progressing, but there were many goals still unattained. I could breathe, but I couldn't swallow one bite of wholesome food. Taking small, shuffling steps alongside someone was nothing like jogging freely. Reacting to a noisy sound or turning my head toward a voice was not the same as talking. Responding to stimuli was one thing—being awake and aware of my surroundings was something else. For all of the visions of healing to be fulfilled— for me to speak in front of a crowd of people about my story of healing—there would have to be more healing ahead. I would need God's healing power, and the prayers of His people, to reach each goal. With that, perhaps God would grant me the wonderful privilege of having a brain alert enough to ponder the mysteries of the angel He had placed by my side during the distress of the accident.

Sunday dawned with a clear blue sky, a beautiful backdrop for a day when people would be gathered outdoors to pray for me. The group of women from Owatonna called MOPS, mothers of preschoolers, organized a second prayer walk, like they had done outside of Hennepin County Medical Center. They spread an announcement through social media, inviting people to gather at the front pavilion of Bethesda Hospital at 2:00 p.m.

Before everyone arrived for the event, my family came to visit me. It was Jason and our children, plus my parents, as well as a few others, including my brother Dan and his wife, Beth. I don't remember their visit because I was still staring straight at people without recognizing them openly. It was as if I was an oddly restless person who was apparently awake but not really awake at all.

My mother and Kyra decided that they would again sing the songs I'd learned as a child: "Two Little Eyes" and "The Cannibal King." They hoped that I would hear those silly songs and not only be entertained but also have a burst of youthful energy. They started to sing about the Cannibal King, turning toward me as they found their pitch. My mother and Kyra sang, "The Cannibal King with the brass nose ring fell in love with the dusty maiden."

Then they looked. I was mouthing the words! I wish I remembered this crazy, happy moment! "Ah-ump (kiss, kiss), ah-ump (kiss, kiss), ah-um, ditty-a-di-ada!"

As they kept going, my lips kept moving. I wasn't making a sound, but I mouthed the lyrics of the entire song with them. My mother was astonished, and as she watched me, she saw my brother Dan crying behind me. My father was tearing up too. Tears of joy glistened on their faces as they looked at my face, seeing in my eyes a little more of the Shannon they knew trying to emerge. Then, their episode of true bliss turned into another unforgettable moment that my mother recorded in her journal.

Mom's Journal
I was wearing a sweatshirt with the hood strings hanging down. You were playing with them, and I was talking to you. All of a sudden Jason said you were trying to tie my strings.

You started with crossing them in an X and then quickly continued into the most perfect bow I have ever seen. Again tears of joy! You have never seen a more proud mama!

My mother's delight continued as she kept her eyes on me. Jaydalin handed me one of her stuffed animals, and I held onto it. Then, with Braylon standing in front of my chair, I shook the stuffed bear, kissed it, and gave it to my son. My family was focused and filled with expectation, hoping that I would wake up fully out of my foggy limbo. The minutes passed quickly, and it was time for the prayer walk.

As the MOPS group had done at the previous prayer walk, they brought yellow balloons, a bright gesture of support that speckled the skies with cheerful color. On them, they wrote words of inspiration and Scripture verses. They had invited people to come prepared to pray but not to expect to see me, since no one knew how my condition would be that day. That afternoon, my family decided the fresh air and the momentous occasion would be good for me, so they wheeled me outside to the pavilion where people were gathering. I don't have any recollection of the event, but I stared at the activity as eighty people walked along the pathway near the pavilion and prayed for me and the other patients at Bethesda Hospital.

I sat in my wheelchair as people paused in their prayers, greeting me. They were thrilled to observe that my smile was already less hesitant than it had been twenty-four hours ago, and as they came closer to me, I even extended my hands to them. I readily accepted hugs, and the mood became celebratory for the people attending.

Interwoven with their prayers, they also sang, praising God with their voices, declaring that only He could care for me and bring me to a point of genuine healing. While I sat in my wheelchair, my unsightly scalp covered with a bright green scarf, the group began to sing "Oceans," and then they looked. I was trying to mouth the words.

And I will call upon Your name
And keep my eyes above the waves
When oceans rise, my soul will rest in Your embrace
For I am Yours and You are mine

I couldn't sing, nor was I able to keep up with all of the lyrics, but it was obvious to those watching me that my soul was reaching out to God, resting in His embrace in the ocean of my calamity. As my friend Kristi Hedstrom, who wrote the CaringBridge® posts, later told me, she knew that I was back. Healing was happening. As she saw it, the whole day had the tinge of a miracle.

It was a gradual miracle, just like God had seemed to indicate to so many people. There were still many obstacles to overcome, but there was no doubt for the people looking at me that Shannon was still Shannon. I don't remember that day, but other days would come when I would gain more clarity—mental clarity as well as clarity surrounding the entire extraordinary experience.

My mother capped off the amazing day with a comment that hinted at the impact of everything that had happened. There were eighty people at the hospital that day to pray, and countless people had already visited me throughout the prolonged days of vigil.

Mom's Journal
The hospital keeps saying you are a very popular person! You get so much company.

The company came as friends and also as observers of something unusual that was beyond me. God was not only demonstrating His healing power in my life personally but also making Himself known through the prayers of many people. People were amazed to see how real God is, and there was an irresistible urge to be nearby as God answered their prayers, day by day. The miracle was not over.

Sunday had been momentous for my family and for the many other people who saw me. For me, it was all a blur. Monday was another blurry day, one day closer to waking up completely. To pick up the pace of my healing, the hospital increased the frequency of my therapy sessions. Twice daily I was in both physical and occupational therapy, in addition to speech therapy. I wasn't ready to talk yet, but the hospital staff was preparing my mind and mouth to regain the capacity to communicate verbally.

My basketball skills, though, seemed to be serving me well under the surface of my indefinable lack of awareness. In therapy on Monday, I caught a ball and then threw it back. When I scored some points by tossing small beanbags into a basket, Jason caught the action on video with his cell phone. I was no basketball star, but Jason was a captivated cameraman, thrilled with every tiny triumph.

Kristi reported on the CaringBridge® site that I was improving by leaps and bounds. If only I would leap back into a normal state of consciousness! But progress in other areas was undeniable.

I climbed up and down four steps with a therapist supporting me, and then I walked along a wall holding a railing all by myself. In my task-oriented therapy sessions, I loaded toothpaste onto a toothbrush and brushed my teeth. I also practiced getting in and out of a car in the hospital therapy gym, not flinching at being behind the wheel again.

My family was happy to see that the prospect of my going home from the hospital, even doing housework, was not an impossibility. When Braylon watched a video recording of a therapy session where I was folding and stacking towels, he smiled and quipped, "Now Mom will be able to do our wash." Then, when the therapists handed me a shirt to fold, Braylon said, "She won't know how to do that because we hang our shirts up." The video continued, and Braylon laughed as he saw me throw the shirts at Jason.

Medically, my body was getting into a better rhythm, and they removed my urinary catheter, enabling me to use the bathroom for the first time in eight weeks. The doctors also inserted a plug on my tracheostomy tube, preparing me for its eventual removal and prompting me to breathe only through my mouth and nose. My ability to swallow lagged, though, and the sluggishness of my throat muscles was a stubborn barrier that loomed over the momentum of my recovery.

But, as Kristi typed into the blog post, "This woman is determined!" And even though I was still unaware of my status, I seemed to know who I was. I wrote my name that day—Shannon!

WEDNESDAY
November 11, 2015

As the overall pace of my healing accelerated, my mother's journal entries became a series of upbeat news flashes. She tracked the small things I was accomplishing and, day after day, paused to thank God for the big things that He was doing.

Mom's Journal

You are playing catch back and forth, going faster and faster. You are walking better and stronger every day! So proud of all your accomplishments, girl. You rock, and with the Lord working for you and with you, you are going to be unstoppable! *Whose report do you believe? We shall believe the report of the Lord. His report says you are healed! His report says you are filled. His report says you are free. His report says victory!* And we are walking toward victory! Lord, thank You for everything You have done! We ask that You continue to heal her and please give her the ability to swallow. You have brought her so far. I know You are walking on this journey right beside us. Thank You so much for holding our hands.

THURSDAY
November 12, 2015

My brother Tim, who is the one in the middle of the three, came to see me on Thursday, along with his wife, Tasha. Tim later told my family that the most heartening part of their visit happened when he was telling me stories. Tim's excitement was based on one observation: I had laughed! That became the headline of the next CaringBridge® post because where there is laughter, there is life. I'm glad that Tim's funny stories triggered that instinctive response, stirring up a twinkle of laughter between brother and sister. Laughing with the people I love is one of life's biggest pleasures.

FRIDAY
November 13, 2015

Kristi reported on the CaringBridge® site that I kept pushing myself to take longer strides and increase my speed with each step. Yes, that sounds like me.

My family kept me occupied with stimulating activities to awaken my mind. They lost track of how many games of checkers we played. I was able to move the pieces around the board, although I did break the rules of the game, ignorant that I was cheating. My naive strategies to win hardly mattered to anyone because the fun itself was a huge success.

From what my family tells me, it was as if I were awake, but not to full capacity. I was crawling out of the coma, able to do some things while stunted in other areas. Somehow, though, I was engaged in my surroundings enough to know that Bethesda Hospital was not where I belonged. I was on a journey of healing that would take me further. Brain trauma had no hold on me—God held me firmly, not allowing me to drown in this crisis. As my favorite song says, *Your grace abounds in deepest waters, Your sovereign hand will be my guide.* My mother jotted in her journal one episode that day that indicated I was eager to be done with the agonizing ordeal.

Mom's Journal
Steph and Katie were with you, and you were writing on and off during the day. As the day went on, you were making it very clear you wanted to leave with them. You wrote, "Take me when you go."

I remember that! I really do vaguely remember this instant when my eagerness to be healed clashed with the fact that there were still obstacles ahead of me. I wanted to overcome every obstacle. I remember sitting in my wheelchair that day, thinking, *How am I supposed to get out of here?* I had been in a hospital for exactly two months. *How do I sneak out of here? I can't walk; I can't even eat.*

And then I looked at Stephanie and Katie and thought, *When you leave, take me.* So, I struggled to write that on a piece of paper, desperate to bounce back to living like I had before the collision, when I could run outside so fast that no one could catch me. Outside of the hospital, back at home, I could be with my family and love them like I always had. But I couldn't yet. When my friends left and didn't take me, I was mad at them. I really didn't get it.

It was all so confusing. I wanted to communicate, but my mind was restricted. I could barely eke out a single word. And although I do remember my desire to escape from the boundaries of the hospital and bypass my current mental capacity, my brain was still foggy. I don't remember hardly anything during these post-coma days.

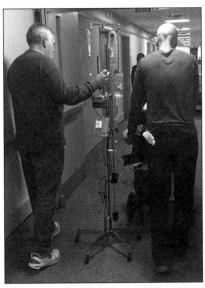

Shannon in wheelchair with Jason and Dad

My family, though, loves to recount the series of firsts during the days of mid-November. Each one of them has a memory of a moment, or two or three, when the Shannon they knew emerged a little more. Jason and our children visited me on Sunday afternoon, and they were excited when they noticed me interacting with them individually. I seemed to know who each of them was, hugging Jaydalin and Kyra, high-fiving Braylon, giving Trenton a thumbs-up. The climax for Jason was when I grabbed his cell phone, looked intently at the keyboard as if I were about to send a text message, and punched with my fingers: *I love u.*

My parents were there too, delighted with one smile after another as I expressed affection for each person gathered around my chair. They knew that I was still struggling to surpass each hurdle, mustering as much pluck as I could. My mother captured that exertion in her journal, logging each of the firsts and recognizing that each first came because of my fight to win.

Mom's Journal

When we were in the room and you were coughing and working hard to get it up, you motioned for a pencil. You wrote, "I have got this!"

What about the prognosis that I would only stare blankly at a wall? Jason had chosen not to pull the plug on me in the first week after the accident, against the recommendations of the doctors. They thought I would turn into nothing more than a vegetable, but here I was sending a text message about love.

One of the doctors who had warned Jason that I would most likely never recover stopped by my room occasionally throughout the weeks of my hospitalization. She hadn't seen me for a while. On this day, I was sitting up straight in a chair, and Jason was next to me as the doctor entered my hospital room. I looked at the doctor and made eye contact with her. Then I waved, a friendly hello.

The doctor was astonished, and Jason watched her reaction, realizing that this skilled doctor was standing in front of tangible evidence of God's healing power. According to what the doctor knew from a medical standpoint, my alertness was physically impossible. She could hardly believe that she was looking at the same woman who, just weeks before, had suffered a severe brain injury. Jason, however, had believed all along that I would not be brain-dead forever, even though the doctors thought he was mistaken. He was neither crazy nor ignorant—he was full of faith that Jesus would heal me. And as the doctor stepped away that day, still shocked, Jason was thankful that God had given her an unforgettable opportunity to look into the eyes of a miracle.

I wasn't sleeping well, which is typical for brain trauma patients. I went back and forth between restlessness and fatigue, but I was still pressing toward the goals that had been established for my recovery. Going up and down a full flight of stairs was easier for me than swallowing. And if I couldn't swallow, I couldn't eat. Swallowing was still extremely difficult because even sucking on ice chips could suddenly trigger a coughing spell.

My voice was extremely weak, so my family had to strain their ears to comprehend my faint words. Within the past few days, Jason had heard me say "yes" in response to a question, but overall, anything I tried to verbalize had only been flimsy attempts to communicate. Finally, though, I was starting to talk loudly enough that they could hear me. My mother took note of something I said that offered a glimpse into my cloudy perspective about my condition.

Mom's Journal

You said to me, which I think is a really good thing, that you just need to get your memory back. I know it will continue to come back. You are doing amazing, and the Lord is totally restoring you! Just pray and believe and be patient! We love you so much!

My childhood friend Mandy Spinler remembers an unforgettable moment that she had with me as I was coming out of the coma and beginning to talk. She visited me at Bethesda Hospital that day, after not having seen me since I was in the ICU at Hennepin County Medical Center, and the gloomy darkness had now lifted. This time I was contributing to the conversation. In fact, I was the one reminding her of something that had happened when we were younger.

We played basketball together and ran cross-country, and Mandy flat-out admits that I was always faster than her. Mandy was fast, too. When I came in first place, she was always second. There was a cross-country race in junior high when we were both running, and as we sped along, clearly in position to place first and second, I slowed down a little bit to let Mandy catch up to me.

Longing to get the first-place medal just once, Mandy called out to me as she ran up from behind. "Please, can I win this time?" she gasped.

I took off, sprinting faster than ever. As I raced ahead, I cried out over my shoulder to Mandy, "No way!"

That day in the hospital, I was laughing and laughing, bringing up that old story. Oddly enough, I don't remember that conversation now, but Mandy has since shared how momentous it felt to her, hearing me laugh and talk. She didn't care anymore about first or second place. What mattered to her was that I was not only alive, but I was still the Shannon she knew. She was happy that my competitive spirit, and my friendship, had not diminished at all.

But of course, coming out of the coma was still a battle. On Thursday, I was confused most of the day and only slept about an hour. After all those weeks of incessant sleeping, I was only slowly getting back in sync.

Maybe my brain was tired from the exertion of the previous day, when my brother Tim came to visit me again, this time setting me up with an iPad so that I could send text messages whenever I was able to reach that point of communication. Apparently, I was ready. On Wednesday, I had surfaced on the screens of a handful of family and friends, texting a few short words. The most significant was when Jason texted me a question, asking how many years we had been married. He saw my prompt reply pop up on his cell phone: 16. How I could answer that question about the past without remembering my present-day activities? That is something I can't explain. My brain was doing its best, and in between all of these efforts, I needed a lot of rest.

Still not exactly aware of everything, I began to recognize people more and more. I don't remember those lightbulb moments, but I do have a vague memory of looking at people. They would look at me, and they would be crying, while I sat there wondering why they were crying.

My mother-in-law, Kristine, came to visit me at the hospital, along with my mother, Kyra, and Jaydalin. They stopped by after school, and as they joined me in the patients' family visiting area, Kristine FaceTimed her daughter Marcie. I was playing with my girls, and Kristine's cell phone seemed to distract me. Abruptly, I turned and reached out for it. My mother watched as I took the phone from Kristine's hands.

Then I looked at the cell phone screen and said, "Hi, Marcie Lynn!" That's the name I always use for Jason's sister. Marcie was so overwhelmed with joy that she started bawling, and although I don't remember any of the specifics, I remember the tears of moments like this. My mother played a part in the emotional episode and wrote about it in her journal.

Mom's Journal

A big thing for me is that you know you aren't there yet, which means it will get there. You were telling Marcie all the things you couldn't do, and I stopped you and said, "Tell her all the things you CAN do!" So you smiled and started listing off the things you could do! Love it! You are doing amazing, and God ain't finished with you yet.

Immediately after writing that in her journal, my mother added another paragraph, her large, fluid handwriting showing her excitement. Clearly, my healing was on the verge of becoming something bigger than anything I could have dreamed while I was sleeping in the coma.

Mom's Journal

You already have two churches waiting for you to come and speak, and that is just the beginning of the completion of the vision the Lord gave to four people to give to us in the beginning of our faith walk healing journey. God has been so faithful! And so many times I remember Mike Ramsey's word to you around Memorial Day weekend. "Shannon, don't be afraid." And we wondered what that meant. Well, now we know what it meant, and the Lord has walked with us every step of the journey and will bring us through to completion!

Forging ahead with my therapy sessions and trying to swallow was no game, but I did play plenty of games. On Saturday, my mother and Kristine came again with Kyra and Jaydalin. My daughters and I put makeup on each other and played games together. It was a fun way to pass the time in a tough situation, while the clock kept ticking in God's perfect timetable for my recovery.

SUNDAY
November 22, 2015

On Sunday, Jason talked with me about the accident. He had mentioned it to me before, but I was still not grasping what had happened and didn't know why I was in the hospital. That realization would come later for me, and when it came, I would not forget it.

In the meantime, I expressed concern when hearing that Kyra and Jaydalin had been in the van with me on that fateful morning and had been impacted by the collision. Jason had to reassure me that the girls were doing great. I seemed relieved to hear that Jaydalin had hardly been harmed and that Kyra had been healed. The pieces were starting to come together in my mind, and in the big puzzle of what God was doing through the whole experience. There were still some pieces missing, though, until I would have a story to tell.

MONDAY
November 23, 2015

One more goal down, several more to go! On Monday, the doctors removed my tracheostomy tube and covered the small hole in my neck with gauze. As that skin was starting to heal, I expressed that my next goal was to move on from my feeding tube so that I could eat. Apparently, I told people that I wanted pizza! I just deny it with a smile now because I never beg for junk food like that, but they insist that is what I said. In speech therapy, I swallowed three ice chips, a significant feat because swallowing anything was going to be harder than I had thought.

My physical strength was increasing, and my strides were longer as I walked on the treadmill in therapy for two five-minute stints in a harness that day. It was obvious that I was motivated to push myself, and I also seemed impatient to get going! My progress prompted the staff at Bethesda Hospital to submit paperwork for me to be transferred to another facility for therapy that would be even more intensive. They told my family that they hoped to issue the authorization within a couple of days.

TUESDAY
November 24, 2015

On Tuesday, my family received a message that struck them. They realized that all the encouragement they felt as they watched my progress was only a drop in the bucket compared to the ripple effect in the lives of other people. Jason got a message from the uncle of the second police officer who arrived at the scene of the accident, describing how terrible the circumstances had been as Kyra and I sat trapped in the van. The man gave us a very straightforward look at what his niece had experienced when her job as a police officer and her role as a mother converged. He wrote about it to Jason like this:

Police Officer's Story

I don't typically talk to my niece about calls she may have been at, and she typically doesn't share too much, but I was at her home on Halloween, and we started talking about being a mom. She has an eighteen-month-old boy and said that a recent car accident she witnessed has made her decide she may just hang up her uniform. She said what she saw that day made her realize that life can be cut short and in an instant you can lose someone that means the world to you.

I asked her what she saw that made her rethink her career. This is what she said: She was the second officer at the scene, assessing what had happened. They needed to make a decision on who to care for first. As officers, they always want to assist a child; however, the mother was just as bad if not worse than the daughter. My niece checked on the mother and, seeing that she couldn't assist in removing her from the car, went to be with the daughter who was seriously injured. Not to get into too many details, my niece held the little girl as best she could and lifted her head so she could breathe.

In that moment, my niece became a mom and not an officer. She couldn't separate herself from knowing how painful this was going to be for the parents, or at least the dad. She kept thinking about how young this life was and how unfair life can be. She looked over at the mom, who she knew wasn't going to make it as well, and couldn't get over the deep emotional pain that this family was going to go through. When more help arrived, my niece got physically sick and, at that moment, rethought her career. She too had a baby at home that needed a mommy.

As my niece was telling me this story, I began to remember your Facebook post about the accident and then following the entire story on CaringBridge®. I told my niece about the family I had been praying for, and the accident sounded eerily similar. And at that moment we realized it was the same family. I proceeded to bring up the CaringBridge® site on my phone and showed her that not only did the little girl survive, but the mother as well! My niece was overwhelmed with joy and could not believe they survived. She said that it must have been a miracle, and I said, EXACTLY!

This candid message reinforced what my family had known. God had spared Kyra, Jaydalin, and me—it was a miracle. And my family realized, too, that the significance of that extraordinary event was something more magnificent than any of us. We would need to keep walking with God to discover His purpose for preserving our lives.

WEDNESDAY
November 25, 2015

The Bethesda Hospital staff announced to Jason that the day had come for me to move and that it was up to him to drive me to the next facility. I was headed to the Courage Kenny Rehabilitation Institute at Abbott Northwestern Hospital, an intensive rehab program designed to nurture my healing and prepare me for increased levels of independence. Being approved to advance to this stage of my recovery was like getting a gold medal, from the perspective of my family. From my perspective, it was not the kind of progress I wanted. I was still struggling to comprehend things that were happening. When I heard that I was leaving Bethesda Hospital, I thought that meant I was being discharged to stop at a doctor's office and then go straight home.

So, Jason and I got into the van with our minds in different places. He was overwhelmed with the idea of being responsible for transporting me from St. Paul to the new location in Minneapolis. Every other time that I had been shuttled across town, I had been strapped to a stretcher in an ambulance. Now it was just Jason and me, and I seemed so feeble and frail, sitting next to him in the front seat.

I didn't understand that I wasn't going home, but as we drove along, I began to grasp that I was only being transferred. "I'm not going to another hospital," I said. "I'm going home today." My vocal cords were weak, my voice straining to be heard over the hum of the engine.

"Honey, I can't hear you," Jason said, his eyes focused on the road as he drove, trying to guard his delicate passenger from any additional damage. He really couldn't hear me because my voice was so soft. When we arrived at Courage Kenny, one of the staff members greeted us, welcoming me to the new rehabilitation facility. Confused and frustrated, I kept insisting to Jason that I was not staying at that place, and Jason gently tried to tell me that this was where I needed to be.

It was so hard for me to comprehend. "What?!" I said, turning to Jason and adding, "You're not on my team!" I was mad. I badly needed to be there, to go through the next phase of therapy, but I just didn't get it. I didn't understand that I was still unfit for life beyond the walls of the medical facility. After Jason left so that I could settle into my new hospital room, I cried and cried. I was crushed, thinking that I was stuck on a forced vacation in a hotel and wondering why I couldn't go home.

Now I grasp it. I realize how vital those days of therapy were, as my abilities expanded and even skyrocketed. And I also realize that Jason was 100 percent on my team, rallying for me and valiantly playing his part in this awful calamity. In all the days when I was incoherent, he was present and praying, faithful to me and full of faith. He was on my team more than I am even capable of explaining, and I'm grateful.

It was Thanksgiving Day, and I was thankful to be alive, but I didn't really know what day it was. Jason stepped away from our large family gathering, staying by my side during my first full day at Courage Kenny rehab center. Friends supplied our family with the sweet potato casserole and peanut butter pie that I usually make, and others filled in the gaps in the menu and around the table. I didn't know about it until afterward, but I'm sure it was all delicious. I couldn't eat any of it anyway! I texted a little bit with my mother a few times and took a selfie with Jason, seeming to miss being with the crowd. My mother recorded her own impressions of how it felt to be spending the holiday across town.

> **Mom's Journal**
> When you heard it was Thanksgiving, you weren't too sure what that was, but when they explained it, you said, "Oh, I remember that," and then said, "Oh, I guess I can't go this year," and you seemed sad. Well, my girl, you have many more Thanksgivings that you will be at and can enjoy because our Lord planned a miracle for your life so you could bring glory to Him. You are being healed because our God says you are!

I'm certain that there was a strong spirit of gratitude around the dinner table that day, seeing Kyra and Jaydalin eat heartily, alive and thriving wonderfully in the aftermath of the accident. And everyone knew that I was thriving, too, or close to it. Kristi Hedstrom surveyed my friends and family, compiling a post for the CaringBridge® site that was packed with quotations from each one of them. Their expressions of thanksgiving resounded, culminating with these words from Jason, quoted at the end.

CaringBridge® Blog

I am overwhelmed with thankfulness for all the people that began praying for my family on September 14 and have continued to pray and tell others to pray on our behalf. I am also extremely blessed and thankful for every child that decided to lift my bride and daughters up to our heavenly Father. I will never be able to thank each of you enough. Thank You, Christ Jesus, for sparing my wife and daughters.

FRIDAY
November 27, 2015

The staff at Courage Kenny filled my schedule with rigorous therapy sessions aimed at edging me closer to being able to function fully. Therapy kept me occupied, and it also meant that my family didn't need to be quite as vigilant. My mother noted that she spent the day on Friday entertaining Kyra and Jaydalin with a trip to the movies, topped off with pizza. But she never stopped being curious about how I was doing.

> **Mom's Journal**
> I stayed in Owatonna with the girls today, so not sure what all the wonderful things you are accomplishing today, my girl. The girls and I had a fun day!

The heightened sense of concern had eased. My family was no longer waiting to see if I would open my eyes because that vigil was over. I had already looked into their eyes, my brown eyes no longer an empty gaze. What remained to be seen was when I would overcome the remaining obstacles that stood between me and the continuation of the story that God was telling. I still wasn't up to giving any speeches, that's for sure.

SATURDAY
November 28, 2015

My mother even used the word *animated* when describing how I interacted with my children on Saturday. What a difference from the somber, sluggish state that had been my norm for so many weeks. She may not have even realized how her word choice was specifically starting to fulfill what had been foreshadowed right after the accident. My friend Kiki Stapp had been the one to say that eventually I would be speaking to a large group of people on a stage, very animated with my arms. God had given Kiki this shining promise during the darkest days, and soon it would be so.

My father and I played Sequence over and over, passing the time and pushing my brain to think straight. Sequence is a game that was invented in my hometown of Owatonna, Minnesota, in the 1970s, and we had enjoyed it many times when I was younger. Now, in the hospital, we probably played a few hundred games, and it was so much fun. My father was thrilled that I knew what to do, pulling cards from the deck and putting chips on the game board to match each one.

And I remember those evenings! Finally, my brain was forming fresh memories of good times. Finally, my father was beaming next to his competitive daughter, while I tried my hardest to beat him by being the first one to finish a sequence in the game. Finally, my brain seemed to be more aware that life has a sequence, and I was pressing forward.

We don't have a photo of the angel in the van, but we do have a photo of the van wreckage. My mother faced that image for the first time today. The passenger side, the place where I was sitting when the responders found me, was crushed and mangled, the metal shell of the van crumpled like a wad of tissue paper.

Looking at the damage was distressing, but the presence of the fourth person in the vehicle was an amazing sight that still overrides all the anguish. The driver's seat was empty now. There was no lingering trace of the angel who had been slumped over the steering wheel, almost as if bowing to quietly pray. What remained? Through the prayers of many people, we were still alive, guarded by the power of God. This was what we knew so far. For now, it was my mother's turn to jot in her journal her impressions of what she saw.

Mom's Journal
I saw a picture of the van for the first time today. I haven't wanted to see it. Jason didn't know I hadn't seen it and sent it to me in a text. It is horrible, but like Jason said, it's part of the testimony. God has done an amazing work with my three girls, and I will never be able to thank Him enough for saving your lives and bringing you home. It's a huge miracle!

Before long, I would be looking, too—looking at what had happened in that awful collision. Soon I would see more clearly what God was doing with me.

TUESDAY
December 1, 2015

The hospital staff was right when they said that the rehab program at Courage Kenny would be rigorous. It was like a full-time job. I had therapy sessions from 8:30 a.m. to 4:30 p.m., and I was working hard.

Putting pressure on my right heel while standing was tough, and I tended to stand on my tiptoes, straining to regain flexibility. Pushing myself was paying off, though, and I reached the point where I could walk wherever I needed to go in the hospital without having to ride in my wheelchair.

If only I could jump over the hurdle of swallowing, which was still a struggle. So far, I was only practicing by swallowing thickened apple juice, but even taking one small sip was a choking risk.

THURSDAY
December 3, 2015

The doctors performed an X-ray, which revealed why my voice was so soft and why I was having so much difficulty swallowing. My right vocal cord was paralyzed, so eating would have to be put on hold. I was craving my mother's homemade meatloaf! It might be another four weeks before I could even experiment with swallowing any kind of food.

So, I could settle in and wait, or keep trying to beat each goal. Of course, my only option, as I saw it, was to keep fighting toward the finish line. The sooner my vocal cords loosened, the sooner I could speak up and tell my story.

FRIDAY
December 4, 2015

The appearance of a fourth person in the van, perhaps an angel, was already fascinating, but God wasn't finished. The story would go beyond me, beyond the baffling and inexplicable eyewitness account at the scene of the accident. Today my mother's journal brought another glimpse of what God was doing behind the scenes. We would need to stay tuned for further episodes, according to what my mother heard from Aunt Peggy.

> **Mom's Journal**
> Peggy called. Liz was praying, and the Lord spoke to her and said . . . We haven't begun to see what He is going to do! I am so excited! I know His plans for you are huge!

Liz Matson had been praying for me since day one. Living in North Carolina, she was too far away to watch my eyes brighten as I crawled out of the coma, but never too far away to pray. Over 1,000 miles across the country from Minnesota, she believed that God is not limited by distance and that He was with me while she prayed. Those who prayed all over the country and around the world, like Liz, were looking at my calamity through eyes of faith —and seeing God reach down from the infinite heavens to care for me and hold me closely, whispering my name. There was no doubt that God was doing something big—He had sent an angel. God had protected me from death during the collision, and He had more plans for my life.

Part of God's plan meant that our family would forever have a point of connection with other people going through similar situations. No longer would we hear about a tragic car accident without feeling empathy. We knew the pain of the victims, and we knew the struggles of everyone surrounding the calamity. On Friday afternoon, my mother had a terrifying experience that took her back to day one all over again, and she wrote about it after the enormous scare.

> **Mom's Journal**
> I had a horrible thing happen today. I was on my way to school to get your kids, going down 225th Street West on my way to Dodd Road, when a silver pickup came out of control into my lane and back and forth. Then it started to roll, and then someone got ejected from the truck. It rolled again, and someone else got ejected. All the time, I am screaming in disbelief as that truck is flying through the air, coming at my Suburban. I didn't know if I was going to have to drive in the ditch. It stopped twenty to thirty feet away from me. I sat there screaming in horror of what I had just seen. In absolute horror. It was just too close to us going through your accident. In the end, two Lakeville South students died. It was so horrible to watch!

My mother's very first lines in her journal in September had been about day one—a horrible day, as she called it. Now she was reliving the experience from an entirely different angle. She feared for her own life this time, and she agonized over the loss of life that she witnessed. Two Lakeville high school students died that afternoon, and two others survived. One of the survivors suffered minor injuries, and the other one was in critical condition at Hennepin County Medical Center, the same hospital where I had been airlifted that tragic day.

Was there any hope for Alex Hughes, the student who was now hospitalized? My mother saw no angel that afternoon as she looked at the wrecked pickup truck, but she knew that God could turn something so horrible into a story of healing. The wounds of our family's calamity were still raw, but the miracle of my healing created fresh opportunities to encourage others. Soon my mother would exchange her fearful screams for words of soothing comfort, and soon I would join her in bringing a message of hope.

Things were starting to make a little more sense inside my head, but my thoughts fell apart a lot when I tried to express them. I scrambled my words, and sometimes my mind would go blank, fumbling through the pages of my mental dictionary. But at least I was thinking and talking to some extent, and not stuck forever inside a stagnant, broken, traumatized brain and body.

My brain and my body were ready to keep stretching. I wanted to live and join the fun in the world outside the walls of the rehabilitation center. Doing elementary sports drills in therapy was good for my recovery, but I wanted to be back on the basketball court, scoring real points. I also knew that I was missing my children's sports activities, and I longed to be cheering for them. But I couldn't go to their games, nor could I cheer loudly. On Saturday, when I heard that my son Trenton was going to have a basketball game that day, I almost convinced the nurse to let me leave briefly to attend the game. But I had to stay, and Jason had to remind me that resting was more important than anything right now. If I rested now, I could soon be back in the game.

While I was eager to be released from the rehabilitation facility, finally almost at the point where that could be possible, my mother couldn't get Friday's tragedy out of her mind. It wasn't the image of the tumbling pickup truck that bothered her—it was the thought of lost lives and the fact that this athletic teenager who survived was at the beginning of a rough journey like mine had been. She felt compelled to get involved, as she wrote in her journal.

Mom's Journal

I think Dad and I are supposed to go see the kid who got airlifted to HCMC in that accident yesterday. Don't know why

the Lord had me there to see it all happen. But He has to
have a plan here.

Aunt Peggy had just told my mother the day before that God
had big plans for me, and it was no coincidence that my mother
had seen the accident on Friday afternoon. This was only the
start of many more connections that my family would have with
other people in distress, people longing for a glimpse of God's
extraordinary power.

SUNDAY
December 6, 2015

It was another Sunday where I couldn't join my family for our usual lunchtime stop at Jimmy John's for a fresh sandwich in between church and sports activities. But my family was great about visiting me, and I thrived on having so much company.

Jason's aunts, Cindy and Jean, came from Michigan to see me at Courage Kenny, treating me as if I were at a spa by rubbing my feet and painting my nails. They also took me on a walk beyond the boundaries of my room, and my friend Stephanie was with us, too. Since we went farther in the hallways than I could comfortably walk, they pushed me in my wheelchair, and I enjoyed the outing to the maximum, seeing areas of the lower level where I didn't wander on a daily basis. On the way back, we came to an elevator that was out of order. I decided that I could walk up the steps, so I took off, climbing up two flights of stairs and hanging on to Stephanie for extra support. Meanwhile, Jason's aunts lagged behind us, carrying my abandoned wheelchair upstairs. Stephanie and I reached the top and sat down to wait for them. It took them a long time, struggling to hoist the heavy wheelchair all the way up to the floor where my room was. When they finally joined us, I was giggling like a little girl—and so happy to be in first place again.

My mother missed that episode, but she heard about it and was deeply encouraged. She knew that her daughter was still fiery and fun-loving, rising above the challenges, one step at a time. At the same time, she kept thinking about the challenges that the other family was facing at Hennepin County Medical Center, where the one student was still hospitalized. She was perplexed, wondering why God had put her in a position to see the accident, and she felt the urge to visit Alex and his family at the hospital. She later wrote about it after going with my father to the downtown Minneapolis hospital, confronting the familiar stark hallways where the fluorescent lights glared at the surrounding despair.

Mom's Journal

God is so real to me. Going back there is so hard, but I feel that's what God wants us to do! We went down, met with the dad, and talked and prayed with him for about twenty minutes. Lord, I know You have a plan here. Be with them and let them see You through this tragedy. It's all about You, God!

Monday dawned with the prospect of a meeting that Jason would be having that morning with the doctors to discuss the possibility of my release from the Courage Kenny rehabilitation facility. A

few hours later, brilliant light dawned on all of us when they told Jason that I would be discharged on Wednesday. This time I was not going to be transferred somewhere else—I was headed home! I was so excited!

Everyone else was excited too—my family, my friends, the people who had been praying non-stop. The CaringBridge® posts were infused with excitement, and my mother jotted a few lines in her journal right away.

Shannon in wheelchair with Jason and children

Mom's Journal
It is official. You are going home on Wednesday. Discharge is at 11:00 a.m. You are pretty pumped, and so are ALL of us.

The elation was such a contrast to how things had looked at the beginning. During the meeting on Monday morning, the doctors reported to Jason that I had originally been at Level 3 on the scale that measures the deterioration caused by traumatic brain injury, based on the responses of the patient. The point system goes as high as 15, and my meager 3 points had indicated severe disability and an extremely dismal prognosis. This report matched the sobering diagnosis that Jason had heard from the start in September, and it clashed with Jason's firm conviction that I would be healed.

Ultimately, the brain injury report clashed with the power of God to heal me, just like the lyrics of the song that Jason had heard in the live recording on the Friday night after the accident. "I Am Healed" echoed in Jason's mind as he listened to the doctors.

Sickness, you have no power here,
Darkness, you have no power here,
Chaos, you have no power here,
In Jesus' Name.

There was no doubt that such a radical healing had been God's doing. And there was no doubt that the miraculous appearance of the angel during the accident was evidence that God had a bigger purpose in all of this.

TUESDAY
December 8, 2015

We were all in suspense, waiting one more day. Kristi Hedstrom gave the shortest of updates on the CaringBridge® website on Tuesday, saying that she was postponing a more complete post until tomorrow, when I would be home. She did add one more comment, though, urging people to continue supporting me as they had always done. "In the meantime," Kristi wrote, "please do what you do best: keep praying!"

It had been eighty-six days. Yes, it had been eighty-six days, but the nights seemed to outnumber the days. The agonizing crisis, the grueling climb out of a coma, the calendar clogged with one concern after another—all of it was fading away, finally. I was going home. The steady, quiet miracle of healing was as real as the discharge papers that I held in my hand as I left Courage Kenny Rehabilitation Institute.

We were even ahead of schedule. My release was planned for 11:00 a.m., and by 10:15 a.m., I was out the door. Jason drove me home, chauffeuring his smiling bride and trying to make sense of what was happening as we left the hospital behind us. For both of us, it felt like we were taking a newborn baby home from the hospital, and neither of us knows whose joy was greater on that ride from Minneapolis to Lakeville. We were together, and life was before us again, fresh and somewhat frightening.

Life was not the same as when we had last been in Lakeville together. Eventually I could bake chocolate chip cookies again, like I had done the night before the accident, and someday we could shoot hoops on the basketball court again, like we had done since the first day we met. But we could never rewind the clock and escape the crisis that had changed our reality forever. It would be so comforting for life to be normal, like it had been before September 14, but if we went backward, we would lose what we had become. We were different now. God had reached into our normal, everyday lives, and in a phenomenal way had changed everything into an extraordinary, God-honoring experience. And He had done it with an angel.

The extraordinary experience—the angelic appearance at the accident and all of the amazing events afterward—had turned our lives upside down. But it had also turned our hearts to the power of God to sustain, to heal, to save. God had been our only hope during the gloomy darkness of the eighty-six days and nights, and that would never change. The song "Anchor," which had been the soundtrack of Jason's trips back and forth to the hospital, was still a fitting theme weeks later as we drove home.

There is hope in the promise of the cross
You gave everything to save the world You love
And this hope is an anchor for my soul
Our God will stand
Unshakable

Sitting next to Jason as we pulled up the driveway toward the garage, I noticed a row of pine trees that had been planted since the last time I had been home, a gesture of generosity from our friends. Jason told me that they wanted us to have a constant reminder of the new life that God had miraculously given me. The long driveway was wider than I remembered, and I found out that this, too, was the work of our friends, who had reinforced the ground underneath the surface so that our path was firm.

Getting out of the car, I walked toward the house, and my eyes fell on the two wooden chairs painted bright red, to the left of the front door, where they had always been. I would be sitting there soon, just like usual, to think about the things of God. Except that now my perspective would be new. God had not changed, but I had, and I had more to learn about His purposes in my life.

Moe, our English bulldog, who pretends to be a perky watchdog, was as dependable as ever, standing at the threshold of the front entrance. Jason ushered me inside and escorted me throughout the whole house, letting me pause to get reacquainted with each room, and tenderly supporting my small frame as I navigated each step. It was overwhelming, but I was overjoyed.

A few hours later, Jason and I went to pick up the children at school. I was finally fulfilling the promise I had made to my boys on the day of the accident, only this time no one was thinking about the Yorkshire terrier puppy that I had wanted to buy on the morning of the accident. The children were so ecstatic to see me that all of us were torn between happy hugs and glistening tears. The spontaneous burst of emotions made it the best family reunion we could have imagined. Kyra, Jaydalin, and I had been through the collision, while Jason, Trenton, and Braylon had taken the blow along with us—and we had never stopped being Team Kerr.

THE CLARITY

EPILOGUE

Mom's Journal
Got up this morning, and it is so awesome that you are here in your own house. You slept until 9:00 a.m.

My mother's journal continued to flow with firsthand observations because my healing journey was not entirely over yet. I was home, but I wasn't totally independent. We needed my mother's help to keep our active household humming, and she stayed at our house for many months while I was still straining to reach specific goals.

I had been a sprinter, not a marathon runner, and this was the longest race I had ever run. I had to reteach myself to do even the simplest things. When I came home from the hospital, I could walk only short distances, and I couldn't run at all. I was still struggling to swallow ice chips, let alone eat or drink. I could barely talk, and I had to wear earplugs all the time to buffer the noises for my fragile, traumatized brain. I would say one thing and mean something else, as if my brain were a tangle of crossed wires. And, even if I wanted, it was too soon to consider driving again.

It was a real challenge, not a fairy tale, but I was alive—and not a vegetable. Sometimes I did feel rotten, though. I wondered why the accident had happened, wondered what God was doing all along. People had told me about the angel sitting next to me in the van, but I didn't know how to interpret that inexplicable happening. Until more clarity came, I never stopped believing that God had a purpose, and I pressed forward, getting stronger each day. I am essentially a fearless person, not recoiling in adversity. God is always with me, and that is all I need, just like the lyrics of "Oceans" say.

Your grace abounds in deepest waters
Your sovereign hand
Will be my guide
Where feet may fail and fear surrounds me
You've never failed and You won't start now

My recovery during the next several months wasn't glamorous, but it was victorious. I was back to attending my children's sports activities, tucking them into bed at night, and rekindling the motherly affections that had been dormant while I had been comatose. Nurturing my children at an emotional level was harder than I had expected, but it was probably a factor of having focused so much energy on my own survival. My mother said that I acted as if my mercy card were missing, scolding my children more than wrapping my arms around them with grace. Thankfully, that tough period passed, and my close connection to each one of them prevailed.

I loved being surrounded by my family. On my first night at home, I insisted on sitting at the dinner table with them, even though my own nourishment came not from a plateful of food but a feeding tube. The goal of swallowing sometimes seemed insurmountable, and I underwent two procedures to correct the problem with my paralyzed right vocal cord. The gel injection treatments were only partially effective, so I had to keep practicing the basics, one tiny sip at a time. My first taste of real food was January 21—tapioca pudding! It was incredibly delicious to my lonely taste buds! I craved coffee, but liquids would have to come later. I gradually graduated from one food substance to another— Cream of Wheat, thickened Jell-O, sliced bananas. A basic swallow of water was last, after much effort, none of which felt fluid.

On March 23, after overcoming some infections, I was finally freed of my feeding tube. It was just in time to celebrate Easter with my family and join them for a meal of roasted ham, cheesy potatoes, green bean casserole, and mandarin orange Jell-O salad. Easter Sunday was a joyful day for us, gathered around the table and remembering the eternal life that Jesus gave to us through His death and resurrection. We were rejoicing in life like never before. For dessert, we ate strawberries with angel food cake. The fluffy texture of the angel food cake was nothing like the harsh conditions when the angel appeared at the scene of the accident. But there was a certain sweetness in both.

Although I was outside the walls of the hospital and sitting at the family dinner table instead of stuck in a wheelchair, my stint as a recovering patient wasn't over. Right away after arriving home on December 9, I began an outpatient therapy program at Courage Kenny three times a week to increase my mobility and mental agility. By January 11, my results in a balance test had improved by 11 percent, and I was able to walk 150 feet farther than during my previous evaluation. The therapist issued an assessment, stating that I couldn't walk any faster without it being considered running. Ten days later, I was jogging slowly in the hallways during my therapy session, though that hardly counted to me because it was a halting, tentative trot. A more significant accomplishment came a few months afterward, when I ran—really ran.

In July, the six of us—Team Kerr—were attending an outdoor three-on-three boys' basketball tournament at nearby Farmington High School. My children kept begging me to try running, knowing that my legs were itching for a race. I downplayed their idea, saying that I had been trying to run for months with no success. I was too wobbly, too weak. "Just try!" they all pleaded during a break in the tournament. Their prodding nudged me to get back on my feet and try once more, thinking I would probably prove to them again that I really wasn't able to run yet.

So, I stood there, with little Jaydalin by my side, looking up at me expectantly, her cheeks rosy in the summertime heat. Suddenly, Jaydalin took off in a hurry, swinging her arms and scampering as fast as she could. I chased her. I was jogging—and I was thrilled! It was no speed record, but the message that God had sent to my mother through someone who prayed had come true: she will run. I was back to being a runner, and even if I sometimes still feel a little dizzy, I am determined to keep running and carrying the baton, like I did in the relay races around the track when I was a high school student. I have a message to relay, and it's all because of an angel who had opened the gateways of heaven for a miracle.

My first audiences were small and spontaneous. Wherever I went, I had opportunities in conversations to tell people what had happened—how an ordinary drive to Rochester had taken me to an extraordinary crossroad, an intersection with tragedy, where God had intervened and healed me miraculously, beyond any human expectation. There was no way to tell the story without also talking about the fourth person in the van at the scene of the accident. Everyone gets curious when someone says that they saw an angel, and I did my best to explain the inexplicable while I waited to understand it better myself.

One impromptu audience was the neurosurgeon who had seen me twenty-four hours after I arrived at the hospital after the accident, when I was on the edge of death and heaven, and who had also performed the surgery to replace my skull several weeks later. On December 18, nine days after I had been discharged to go home, I returned to Hennepin County Medical Center to have my neck scanned, and the same neurosurgeon saw me. She looked at me and cried. As I told her about the angel in the van and about God's healing hand upon my brain, the neurosurgeon recognized that the accident was a collision between the medical world and the miracles of heaven. She said that my recovery demonstrated the inability of doctors to prognosticate the outcome for a patient with a traumatic brain injury. The tears of this reputable neurosurgeon demonstrated that God had touched her too.

The scan results at the hospital that day were positive, and the doctors cleared me to remove the neck brace that had restricted me for many weeks. I was so relieved that I sent a text to my brothers, saying, "I got to take the stinking necklace off! Good deal!" Before leaving Hennepin County Medical Center in the afternoon, Jason and I went to the pediatric ICU, where Alex, the local high school student who had been driving the pickup truck in the accident that my mother witnessed, was still hospitalized. This time I was the visitor, stopping to see a patient suffering from traumatic brain injury. Jason and I didn't get to be with Alex that afternoon, but we stayed for a few minutes to talk with his father. More than any words of comfort that we could personally offer, we wanted to pray for him. Alex did recover, and he even returned to school. God heals. It was our privilege to pray and pass along our conviction, our hope in the infinite, eternal, unchangeable God of truth.

Then, my audience expanded. After weeks of individual conversations where I struggled to overcome my feeble voice, with background noise drowning out my words, I was getting closer to speaking in a public setting. On Saturday night, February 6, our friends hosted a dinner as a fund-raiser to support our medical expenses, calling it the Team Kerr Family Benefit. About 500 people came! Some of them were people I had known as a child, some were emergency responders, and others were people I didn't even know. A woman in my hometown of Owatonna made T-shirts, selling them to raise funds, so the crowd was all decked out in gray baseball-style shirts with red sleeves. On the front were these words from Matthew 7:7, which boldly states, "Ask and it will be given to you; seek and you will find; knock and the door will be opened to you." Throughout our crisis, Jason's constant cry was an urgent appeal for prayer, and people had rallied—asking, seeking, knocking. They had joined with us in trusting that God would heal me, and the back of the T-shirts labeled each one of them as the tireless team of faithful supporters that we needed: Team Kerr.

The entire evening was overwhelming, and the emotions of everyone in the room swelled when Jason and I took the stage to address the crowd. Jason spoke first, choking up as he remembered how the miracle had begun—day one and all of the distress surrounding the horrible accident. But his downcast posture transformed and his faced tilted upward as he recounted how wonderful it had been to experience the peace that surpasses understanding—and the power of God to heal me. Most of all, Jason wanted to thank people for praying. Then he passed the microphone to me.

I looked at the crowd and said, "Jesus saved my life that day. He healed me! He loves us—every person in this room. All we have to do is love Him back!" I wasn't ready for the standing ovation that my speech triggered, and I really wasn't ready to explain my story more than what I had said. But it was the start of something bigger, just like God had promised.

On April 13, I spoke again, this time more at length, to a group of over 200 women at a church meeting, telling them about God's healing power. It was simple, really. All I had to do was stand on the stage and talk about what God had done for me, how Jesus had saved my life. Then I looked, and as I finished, women were walking toward the front of the auditorium, wanting to pray. My mother was there that day, and both of us were struck by the realization that this was the specific fulfillment of what God had predicted, and many more opportunities would follow. That afternoon, my mother decided that the day had come for her to leave our house in Lakeville, where she had cared for our household for so many months, and return home to Owatonna. It had been hard for her and my father to travel back and forth and barely have any time together, but they did it all wholeheartedly. As she made the transition, she wrote a few lines in her journal.

Mom's Journal

I got back to Shannon's and packed all of my stuff up and loaded the Suburban with all my clothes. I am going home tonight and passing the baton to you, babe. I plan on coming up to get Jayda and the kids at school, stay up there on Mondays, maybe Tuesdays, but go back home at night. I get to sleep in my own bed.

I was ready to press forward to the next phase of my healing and to the next phase of understanding God's purpose for preserving my life. And what about that angel, and all of the other extraordinary encounters? The days were full of more activity, but they were never too full to pause and ponder and pray. The red-painted wooden chairs outside the front door of our home are my favorite spot to pray. It was in May, as the Minnesota weather finally invited me outside again, that I sat in one of those bright red chairs one day and asked God, "Why did You allow this accident to happen?"

Right away, I sensed that God was replying, "Because I knew that you would obey and listen."

"Yes, Lord, I will!" I answered. I understood what God meant. In a fleeting memory, like a faint blip on the machines that were sustaining my comatose body on day one, I vaguely remembered the instant right before the collision.

Then I looked, seeing the semitrailer truck coming toward our van, and cried out to God, "Hurt me, not my girls! I'm the farthest away, but if someone is going to die, let it be me."

What happened next, I can't describe, because I didn't see anything else. All I know is that God spared my life and sent an angel to sit in my seat as the van collapsed into a crumpled shell of metal wreckage. Kyra and Jaydalin survived, and I did as well, my red shirt splattered with blood, my brain damaged severely upon impact as I sat in the passenger seat. The angel was silent, slumped over the steering wheel, wearing a shirt as blue as the clear heavens above us. God reached out in love, putting someone in my place, and I am alive.

Jesus said, "Greater love has no one than this: to lay down one's life for one's friends" (John 15:13). I love my daughters, and I was willing to die so that they could live. But God decided to keep me alive, too, so that I can tell the story of a much greater love—the love of Jesus. I am here on earth only because of Him.

During the gloomy days of darkness, when all that anyone knew was that I was comatose, a lot of very smart doctors said that I was going to die. They said, "Unplug Shannon." Jason, my family, and countless people prayed for me and trusted in Jesus. Well, Jesus healed me, and I woke up. Thank You, Jesus!

Jesus is a healer. He put Himself in our place to save us, to rescue us from sin and death. Jesus died on the cross and rose alive for us! Jesus loves each of us. We just need to love Jesus back—that is it! The extraordinary experience of the angel will always remind me of the love of Jesus, the only one who gives us hope and life. It's a miracle that I am alive, and I live with an eternal hope. And even though I can't explain everything that happened on day one during the accident, or in all of the days of my miracle of healing, I know that I now stand and walk and run high above the crashing storm because of Jesus, just like my favorite song says.

You call me out upon the waters
The great unknown where feet may fail
And there I find You in the mystery
In oceans deep
My faith will stand

In the mystery, I know what matters—the love of Jesus is why I am alive. My mother kept writing in her journal up until September 14, 2016, one year after the accident. Her last few lines confirmed that God's purposes would not be lost on us, because I am now able to fill in the blanks of what happened, and why.

Mom's Journal
I can't believe it's been a year, and what a year it has been. It's been the worst and the best. The worst obviously is the accident and all the horror with that. The best, seeing the Lord move in the miraculous and feeling His presence in such a strong way. And the huge miracle of saving you and Kyra. I think this will be my last entry to my journal story.

Shannon, it's now your story to tell! I wrote all this for you so you would know your story from beginning to end. I love you with all my heart.

My mother's love and the love of all my family and friends have embraced me so much that I can't express my gratitude. They have helped me push forward, and now I have many miles to go to keep running with my story. I will travel far with it, and I'm even able to drive again. On June 9, 2016, I passed a one and a half hour driving test, scoring high in cognitive ability, reaction time, and eye movement. Being back behind the wheel felt good, and I have no fear, because wherever Jesus tells me to go, I will go.

I gained further ground on my feet, too. Just as Jason had predicted, one year after the accident, we went swing dancing like we had done the Saturday night before the extraordinary day that changed everything. I wore the same red dress, laughing and spinning as the music seemed to lift my feet. Then I looked around the room, seeing the man I love and hearing in my mind another tune that both Jason and I now sing. *I am healed, I know I am, for my God says I am.* And I know that I am alive, and I am loved.

I am forever His!

Team Kerr–Kyra-Jo, Jason, Shannon, Jaydalin, Trenton, Braylon

Kerr Family

McCauley Family

To order copies of *Against All Odds*, please go to www.againstalloddsbook.com.

To schedule Shannon for speaking engagements, please visit www.againstallodds.com
or email Shannon at shannon.kerr@againstalloddsbook.com.